Ken
    From one old "Guy"
 to another. Hope you
like it
                Best

9th (AIR) Cavalry Brigade (Provisional)

Combat Operations After Action Report

*III MILITARY REGION
REPUBLIC OF VIETNAM*

1 SEP 1970 - 15 FEB 1971

HILBERT H. CHOLE

MINERVA PRESS
MONTREUX   LONDON   WASHINGTON

**9TH (AIR) CAVALRY BRIGADE (PROVISIONAL)
COMBAT OPERATIONS AFTER ACTION REPORT**
Copyright © Ltc. HILBERT CHOLE (RET) 1995
All rights reserved

No part of this book may be reproduced in any form
by photocopying or by any electronic or mechanical means,
including information storage or retrieval systems,
without permission in writing from both the copyright
owner and the publisher of this book.

ISBN 1 85863 292 7

First published 1995 by

MINERVA PRESS
1 Cromwell Place
London SW7 2JE

Printed in Great Britain by
Antony Rowe Ltd., Chippenham, Wiltshire.

9th (AIR) CAVALRY BRIGADE (PROVISIONAL)

COMBAT OPERATIONS AFTER ACTION REPORT

III MILITARY REGION REPUBLIC OF VIETNAM

1 SEP 1970 - 15 FEB 1971

ABOUT THE AUTHOR

LTC USA (RET) Bert Chole enlisted in the Washington State National Guard in 1954 at the age of eighteen. About a year later, he transferred to active duty as an infantryman and served in the enlisted ranks. In 1964 he graduated from the Infantry Officers Candidate School and was commissioned as an officer in the Army. Having had his fill of walking, he immediately transferred to the Armor Branch.

He served two combat tours of duty in Vietnam; June 1967 to June 1968 and September 1970 to September 1971. Both tours were with the 1st Squadron, 9th (Air) Cavalry, 1st Cavalry Division (Airmobile). The 9th Cavalry is widely known for the amount of combat it saw and for the damage it inflicted on the enemy. At the time of the Vietnam War, the 9th Cavalry was also known (and often looked at askance) for its "attitude". Considered by many to be totally mad, the 9th Cavalry rode to the sound of the guns. The men did so with complete disregard for personal safety and complete disdain for those more conventional military souls who might be foolish enough to get in their way. They may have been unconventional, but they were *very* effective - Cavalry hats, spurs and all!

LTC Chole's combat decorations include: two Silver Stars, four Distinguished Flying Crosses, four Bronze Stars, thirty-four Air Medals and the Republic of South Vietnam Cross of Gallantry with Palm.

His last command before retiring was the 1st Squadron, 17th (Air) Cavalry, 82nd Airborne Division, at Ft. Bragg, North Carolina. He and his wife, Eileen, currently live in Butzbach, Germany, where he is the manager for a Simulator site training soldiers on the M1A1 tanks and Bradley Fighting Vehicles for the US Army.

DEDICATION

Although his name appears nowhere in this After Action Report, LTC John B Stockton had an indelible influence on the formation, tactics and procedures used by Air Cavalry during the Vietnam war. When the 11th Air Assault Division (Test) was formed at Fort Benning, Georgia, in 1965, LTC Stockton was selected to organize and command the first 'Air' Cavalry Squadron in the annals of the Army. It was his vision, Armor officer background, style and cavalry flair that shaped this remarkable organization. Although he had retired from the Army by the time these events occurred, his imprint is on every page of this report.[1]

To the officers and men who were assigned or attached to this provisional brigade, who lost their lives while doing their duty, we, the survivors of that experience, salute you and dedicate this report to you; to honor your unquestioned response to the call of your nation; to honor your courageous deeds, and to let your families know we care and we remember what outstanding men you were.

> *My Captain does not answer, his lips are pale and still,*
> *My Father does not feel my arm, he has no pulse nor will,*
> *The ship is anchored safe and sound, its voyage closed and done,*
> *From fearful trip the victor ship comes in with object won;*
> *Exalt O shores and ring O bells!*
> *But I with mournful tread,*
> *Walk the deck my Captain lies,*
> *Fallen cold and dead.* [2]

---

[1] When the 11th Air Assault Division (Test) was accepted as a viable concept the Division was redesignated the First Cavalry Division (Airmobile) and the Air Cavalry Squadron was redesignated the 1st Squadron (Air), 9th Cavalry. LTC Stockton took the Squadron to Vietnam and was the Squadron's first commander in Vietnam.

[2] Walt Whitman, *Leaves of Grass*

CONTENTS

9TH (Air) CAVALRY BRIGADE (PROVISIONAL) AFTER ACTION REPORT

	Page
Introduction	xi
Letter of transmittal	15
After Action Report	18
1 Sep 70 - 25 Oct 70: (MAP)	35
First Team Combat After Action Report (E Troop)	46
Interrogation Report on the 'Dude'	61
26 Oct 70 - 30 Nov 70: (MAP)	83
1 Dec 70 - 24 Dec 70: (MAP)	94
OPLAN 2-71 (Bob Hope show security)	104
25 Dec 70 (MAP)	108
26 Dec 70 - 30 Dec 70 (MAP)	111
31 Dec 70: (MAP)	114
After Action Report TF Nevins (POW rescue attempt)	118
1 Jan 71: (MAP 1)	138
5 Jan 71: (MAP 2)	139
9 Jan 71 - 31 Jan 71: (MAP 3)	140
1 Feb 71 - 15 Feb 71: (MAP)	150

TAB A
(Decision Paper) 155

TAB B
(Info Paper to G3 on forming provisional Troop) 167

TAB C
(General Order forming E Troop) 194

TAB D
(Manning Chart for E Troop) 198

TAB E
(Lessons Learned in forming a provisional
Air Cav Troop) 206

TAB F
(Results achieved by provisional troops) 220

TAB G
(FRAGO #0297 - 2, 3-17th ACS OPCON to 1 ACD) 224

TAB H
(Request to establish an Air Cavalry Brigade) 228

TAB I
(Mission of the Brigade and Manning of the Bde HQ) 232

TAB J
(Message forming 9th Air Cavalry Brigade) 245

TAB K
(General Order and message forming F Troop) 248

Glossary of Acronyms 257

INTRODUCTION

In March of 1993 I received a letter from CWO-3 (Ret) Lou Rochat, a former member of E Troop, 1-9th Air Cavalry Squadron (I had been the Commanding Officer of the Troop when it was formed), imploring all of us who had been in E Troop to get off our backsides and write about our experiences while in the Troop. Like many veterans of Vietnam I had toyed with the idea of writing about my experiences and have started to do so many times, but the discipline required to write a book was more than the desire I had to devote to such a project. However, Lou's letter was compelling, and I turned to the box of After Action Reports I had written all those years ago (and have been transporting around the world with me since) and I uncovered this After Action Report on the formation of the 9th Air Cavalry Brigade (Provisional) of the First Cavalry Division (Airmobile).

As I re-read those yellow and faded pages I was struck with the fact that this was a historical document that outlined the formation of the very first Air Cavalry Brigade in the US Army and is something that should be shared with historians and those courageous soldiers who were a part of this Brigade. At the time this was written there was nothing unique or different about what we did on a daily basis, in the historical sense; however, twenty-three years after the fact it is very interesting reading and provides an insight into the staff process and tactical employment of Air Cavalry nearly a quarter of a century ago.

The nucleus for the organization of this provisional unit was the 1st Squadron (Air), 9th Cavalry and the driving force that made it happen was the Squadron Commander, LTC (P) Robert H Nevins. Colonel Nevins was highly respected within the 1st Cavalry Division (Airmobile) and his opinion carried a great deal of weight, as well it should, since on his previous command of this Squadron (1967 - 1968) the Squadron and as a result the Division, achieved some of its greatest successes.

There was, and still is, a mind set within the Army that 'Aviators' and 'Aviation units' are support troops. 'They are not really combat types. We call, they haul. They sleep on clean sheets at night, they never get dirty, and they don't know what its like to look down the barrel of an AK-47. They don't understand Infantry or Armor and they certainly aren't capable of commanding those units. They are Aviators for God's sake!'

It was a break with this traditional concept when the Division Commander approved an Infantry Battalion be placed under the Operational Control (OPCON) of this 'Air' Cavalry Brigade (Provisional). Granted it was only for one day and only on one operation, but it was something that had never been done before or, to my knowledge, since.

Perception, regardless of the facts, becomes reality in the mind of any person. The perception was, and still is, that 'aviation units' are not 'combat' units. Well, let's look at some facts.

Using the period from September 1970 to December 1970 we find that this organization was in direct combat with the enemy every day. There were some Infantry battalions and brigades that went months with not a single contact with the enemy. The job of the Army, any army, is to destroy the enemy and his will to fight. You do that by killing and capturing as many of them as is possible and in the process, hopefully, you also destroy their will to fight. Pound for pound, man for man, this unit was the most effective combat organization in the 1st Cavalry Division (Airmobile). In the four month time frame mentioned above;

The combined divisional units killed 762 enemy.

Of the above total the Air Cav Brigade killed 372 of them.

That is 49% of the total killed by the Division but, it was estimated at the time that fully 63% of the Division total kills were initiated by the Cavalry.

During this same period of time the brigade conducted 563 airmobile insertions and 559 airmobile extractions. All, I might add, were combat airmobile operations, for a total of 1122 combat airmobile operations. These ranged from Blue Platoons to Quick Reaction Forces, to Ranger Teams and Combat Tracker Teams, not counting recovery or administrative flights.

During this same period of time our aircraft were shot at 154 times and we had 15 aircraft crash or be destroyed as a result of those firings.

As a scout pilot in this Squadron on my first tour (1967 - 1968) I recall vividly when SSG Wells, my observer and Platoon Sergeant, and I were conducting a low level (that means the skids to the aircraft were about six inches above the highest obstruction) reconnaissance. We popped over a tree line and directly in front of us was an NVA infantry platoon. We were about 100 feet from them and immediately engaged them. SSG Wells was firing his M-60 machine gun as we flew towards them. We flew to within 15 feet of them and I recall thinking, "this is it", we were going to die in the next couple of minutes. We had killed about ten or fifteen of them and I was looking at two NVA soldiers with their weapons on full automatic, firing at us. I recall seeing the heat waves coming off their barrels when suddenly Sergeant Wells' machine gun jammed. I jammed left pedal and pulled in as much power as I could to get out of there. Neither of us nor the ship was hit!

Every Scout Pilot got eyeball to eyeball with the enemy and every pilot in an Air Cavalry unit has looked down the barrel of an AK-47 or a 12.7 anti-aircraft machine gun, or a 57mm anti-aircraft gun, or has had an RPG fired at him. So much for perceptions.

Contained within these pages are five years of Air Cavalry and Airmobility combat experience condensed into a brief six month period. There were many hard lessons learned on how to do it, but we learned and learned well. I am afraid that our experiences and the lessons we learned have been forgotten. The organizational structure of the Air Cavalry Troop and Squadron, depicted herein, no longer exists. The most effective combat unit in an Airmobile or Light Infantry Division has been bludgeoned into a radically different organization. The 'Aviation' experts fine tuned a proven organizational structure to 'improve' its effectiveness.

When I was the Squadron Commander for the 1st Squadron (Air), 17th Cavalry in the 82nd Airborne Division (1976 - 1978) I had the largest battalion sized unit in the division, over 1300 men. Today that same Squadron has 351 authorized spaces and that is referred to as 'fine tuning' an organization.

I served two tours in Vietnam with this remarkable and unique organization (1st Squadron (Air), 9th Cavalry) and was privileged to bring the Colors and a small detachment of men back to Fort Hood when we were ordered to return from Vietnam. As with most personnel who served in Vietnam, that period of time was the defining point in our lives. For those of us in Air Cavalry, with our black Stetsons and 'ride to the sound of the guns' attitude, we knew we were making aviation history and we knew (pound for pound, man for man) we were the most effective combat organization to emerge from the Vietnam war.

I have reproduced this document as it was written. I have added some editorial comments in an effort to clarify some points, but what you have in your hands is the After Action Report, as it was submitted. I should add, that since I was the E Troop Commander and the Brigade S3 during this period, I wrote much of the material that is contained in this report. There are a thousand individual stories contained within these pages and I struggled to refrain from telling some of those stories as I retyped these pages.

LTC (Ret) Hilbert H Chole
Butzbach, Germany
August 1993

DEPARTMENT OF THE ARMY
HEADQUARTERS, 1ST SQUADRON (AIR) 9TH CAVALRY
1ST CAVALRY DIVISION (AIRMOBILE)
APO San Francisco 96490

AVDARS - 1   12 April 1971

SUBJECT: Air Cavalry Brigade Operations

1. This Squadron recently compiled the data concerning the formation and employment of the largest grouping of Air Cavalry the Army has known. This group was a de facto Air Cavalry Combat Brigade and we have recorded our observations and lessons learned while conducting operations with eight Air Cavalry Troops, two Ground Cavalry Troops, a Ranger Company and a Combat Tracker Team. The report as you receive it has no official sanction; however, it can serve some purpose to those following the footsteps of the 'First Team'. This document was officially submitted to the 1st Cavalry Division, prior to the Squadron being reassigned to the 1st Aviation Brigade on 10 April 1971. There has been no official comment returned.

2. As so often happens when administrative reports are compiled in the midst of actual combat operations, the most important lessons are overlooked. While omitted in the report, we must emphasize two important points.

    a. The proposed combination of the Attack Helicopter Battalion with the Air Cavalry Squadron within the Air Cavalry Brigade is extremely important. Air Cavalry must operate with maximum fuel and go light on ordnance to increase time for visual reconnaissance in the operational area. On the other hand, the Attack Helicopter Battalion operates with maximum ordnance since time on station is not as important as the firepower it delivers. This concept was proven time and time again in the 1st Air Cavalry Division which used its Aerial Field Artillery to provide that additional fire power.

    b. There are pros and cons about arming the LOH with the

minigun. It is my opinion, after observing the Scout with and without the minigun, that the minigun is a hindrance to the Scout. First, if the minigun is mounted, there is one less crew member on the aircraft. This reduces the 'Visual Reconnaissance' capability of the Scout by one third. Second, with the minigun mounted, there is a tendency on the part of the Scout to use his aircraft as a 'gunship', again reducing the VR capability of the Scout.

3. Our hope in compiling the attached report was to assist in the formation of the Air Cavalry Combat Brigade at Fort Hood. We are willing to provide any additional data that may be available.

/s/ Carl M. Putnam
/t/ LTC Armor
   Commanding

DISTRIBUTION:
CG, 11 Field Force, USARV, Vietnam
CG, USACDC, Fort Belvoir, Virginia
CG, Project MASSTER, Fort Hood, Texas
CG, USA Aviation Center, Fort Rucker, Alabama
CG, 1st Cavalry Division (AM), Vietnam
CG, Tricap Division, Fort Hood, Texas
CG, USA Armor Center, Fort Knox, Kentucky
CG, 3rd Brigade, 1st Cavalry Division (SEP), Vietnam
CG, 1st Aviation Brigade, Vietnam
Director of Army Aviation, DACSFOR, Washington D.C.
USA, III Corps MACV
CO, 12th Combat Aviation Group, 1st Aviation Brigade, Vietnam
Director, Doctrine Directorate, USACDC, Fort Belvoir, Virginia
CO, USACDC, Armor Agency, Fort Knox, Kentucky
Chief Armor Branch, OPO, Department of the Army
COL Gilbert R. Reed, HQ USACDC, Fort Belvoir, Virginia
COL Robert H. Nevins Jr., 9th ROK Division, Vietnam
COL William R. Cearan, DACSFOR
LTC Jack W. Anderson, DCSOPS
LTC Ronald T. Walker, DACSFOR
LTC Robert F. Mollinelli
MAJ Robert G. Maxson, US Army Armor School, Fort Knox, Kentucky
LTC Billy Williams, 3rd Squadron, 17th Cavalry, Vietnam
BG Conrad L. Stansberry
LTC Lewis E. Beasley

DEPARTMENT OF THE ARMY
HEADQUARTERS, 9TH CAVALRY BRIGADE
(PROVISIONAL)
1ST CAVALRY DIVISION (AIRMOBILE)
APO San Francisco 96490

AVDARS - 3   23 MARCH 1971

SUBJECT: Combat After Action Report

THRU: Commanding General
1st Cavalry Division (Airmobile)
APO San Francisco 96490

TO: See Distribution

1. DATES OF OPERATION: 1 September 1970 to 15 February 1971

2. LOCATION: III Military Region, Republic of Vietnam

3. COMMAND HEADQUARTERS: 1st Squadron 9th Cavalry

4. REPORTING OFFICER: LTC Carl M. Putnam

5. BACKGROUND

   a. In July and August 1970, the First Cavalry Division was responsible for an area of operations that totalled approximately 4536 square miles. The Division staff studied several proposals that would have enabled the Division to increase surveillance over this vast area. On 23 August 1970 a decision paper was published which outlined four courses of action (Tab A). Course of Action 4, which recommended organizing a fourth and fifth Air Cavalry Troop in the 1-9 Cavalry, was adopted in part. The 1-9 Cavalry submitted recommendations to implement this course of action (Tab B). This recommendation outlined the minimum personnel and equipment that would be required to establish the fourth Air Cavalry Troop in the Squadron. On 1

September 1970, E Troop (Provisional) was formed (Tab C). D Company 227th Aviation Battalion was used as the nucleus for the formation of the new troop. Equipment and personnel were assigned or attached from other units within the Division (Tab D). On 20 October 1970 the Troop Commander submitted the lessons learned from the formation of this first provisional Air Cavalry Troop (Tab E).

In December another provisional troop was formed, F Troop. In retrospect, the important lesson learned from the formation of F Troop was that an experienced Air Cavalry Troop Commander should train and organize the troop. Subsequent provisional Air Cavalry Troops were formed within the Brigade but E Troop met with singular success primarily because of the Armor and Air Cavalry experience of the Troop Commander. A comparison of the results achieved for the first three months of operation for each provisional Air Cavalry Troop illustrates the validity of this observation (Tab F).

b. On 26 October 1970, the 3rd Squadron 17th Cavalry was placed under operational control of the 1st Cavalry Division. At that time the 1st Squadron 9th Cavalry was designated as co-ordinator of all Air Cavalry assets within the 1st Cavalry Division's area of operations (Tab G). On 5 November 1970 the 1st Squadron Ninth Cavalry requested permission to establish a provisional Air Cavalry Brigade (Tab H). A follow-up document was submitted to augment the original request. This document outlined the mission, task organization and staff requirements to form the provisional brigade (Tab I).

c. On 5 December 1970, a division FRAGO was published, forming the 9th Air Cavalry Brigade (Provisional) (Tab J). On this same date another FRAGO was published, forming F Troop (Provisional) 1st Squadron 9th Cavalry. D Company 229 Aviation Battalion was the nucleus of this troop with Division units contributing equipment and personnel (Tab K). Concurrent with the formation of these provisional units, the First Aviation Brigade formed E Troop (Provisional) 3rd Squadron 17th Cavalry. The 334th Attack Helicopter company was the nucleus of this organization. It should be noted that during this entire period the 3rd Squadron 17th Cavalry was minus C Troop. The Squadron was also minus D Troop until 31 December 1970.

6. COMMAND AND CONTROL:

a. The vast majority of the time this Provisional Brigade was in existence, it operated without the benefit of a Brigade Commander.

* Author's Note: While the above sentence is technically true a student of this publication should be aware that LTC Robert H Nevins, the commander of the 1-9 Cavalry, was on the promotion list to Colonel. LTC Carl M Putnam arrived in the country and when the Provisional Brigade was approved he assumed command of the 1-9 Cavalry and LTC Nevins was in fact the Brigade Commander during most of this Brigade's existence.

This arrangement posed no problems because of the prior training of the officers involved, the majority of which were Armor Officers. Armor branch training stresses the Task Force concept from the Basic Course through the Advanced Course and the concept is practiced in the field. There were several occasions during this reporting period when the Commander of the 3-17 Cavalry Squadron commanded more 1-9 troops than 3-17 Troops, yet there was never any friction. The TF concept is habitually used in the conduct of Air Cavalry Brigade operations and has proven highly successful.

b. In order to begin a discussion on the Command and Control procedures used within the Air Cavalry Brigade, the normal method of Air Cavalry Troop employment must first be reviewed and understood. During the reporting period the Air Cavalry Troops of this Brigade initiated 67% of all actions within the First Cavalry Division. The objective of the last sentence being: Air Cavalry is not a support element, but is usually the initiating element in the vast majority of this Division's contacts. As such, the term support should only be used in the same context we use it when we discuss one fire team of a rifle squad, providing fires to assist the movement of the other fire team in the squad. Air Cavalry cannot be considered as general aviation support. It must be thought of as a maneuver element in the third dimension.

c. Air Cavalry Troops are not attached or assigned to other maneuver elements. The Air Cavalry Troops must remain under the control of the Squadron Commander to be totally effective. In a fast moving and fluid situation the Squadron Commander must be able to cross attach and reinforce any troop that has located the enemy. If a troop is attached, assigned, or placed OPCON to another maneuver element the Air Cavalry Commander has lost his flexibility and ability to develop the situation and influence the course of action.

d. Each Air Cavalry Troop is assigned a Tactical Area of Operations (TAOR). This TAOR should always coincide with a Brigade area of operations. To facilitate a co-ordinated effort of operations, the Air Cavalry Troop must place a Liaison Officer (LNO) in the Tactical Operations Centre (TOC) of the Brigade they work with. This LNO co-ordinates clearances, areas of interest, aero rifle platoon insertions and necessary fire support. In addition to the above, he keeps the Brigade informed on what the troop has located. In order of priority the troop conducts Visual Reconnaissance (VR) as requested by Division, Squadron, Brigade and that which is generated within the troop itself.

The point to be made here, is that the Air Cavalry Commander, directs the realignment of Squadron assets. To attach or place a troop OPCON (Operational Control) to another maneuver element would require the Air Cavalry Commander to get permission from the Division Commander to release the Air Cavalry Troop from its attached or OPCON status. This is too restrictive and does not allow the Air Cavalry Commander the flexibility to respond to rapidly changing situations.

e. Through the five years of Air Cavalry experience in this Division it has been proven time and again that maximum results are achieved when Air Cavalry is employed in the reconnaissance role. Rapid response to what the Air Cavalry has located is the key to success on the battlefield. This rapid response is called 'Pile On'. A normal sequence of events is as follows:
   A VR team, one Cobra and a Light Observation Helicopter (LOH), (Pink Team) are directed to an area of interest. The Scout detects personnel, bunkers, buildings or indications that the area is occupied.

The team attempts to develop the situation by conducting reconnaissance by fire. If the enemy exposes his position by returning fire or by moving, the team will either attempt to destroy the force with fire power or attempt to further develop the situation by fire or by inserting the Aero Rifle Platoon (Blues). The Blues are inserted to conduct ground reconnaissance to develop the situation. Before the Blues are put on the ground a nearby Rifle Company must be designated as the Ready Reaction Force (RRF). Once designated the RRF, a Quick Reaction Force (QRF) is designated. This QRF is normally a Rifle Platoon from the RRF Company. The QRF must be in pick-up zone (PZ) posture for immediate employment.

*Author's Note: This meant that the QRF was not performing some other mission. They selected a cleared area near where they were operating, moved to it, designated the area as a pick-up zone, placed out security and waited. When the QRF was picked up and inserted, the remainder of the Company (RRF) moved into PZ posture just as the QRF had before them.

After the Blues were inserted the UH-1H (lift) Aircraft from the Air Cavalry Troop laager at the PZ where the QRF is located or as near as possible to the QRF. If the Blues establish contact the QRF is alerted and the Air Cavalry lift aircraft inserts them into the area to link up with the Blues. At this time the RRF must move to PZ posture. Once the QRF is inserted they maneuver with the Blues to further develop the situation. Up to this point the operation is still controlled by the Air Cavalry Troop commander. If this force encounters stiff resistance, the RRF is inserted into the contact area. Once the RRF is on the ground, or at a mutually agreed upon time, control of the operation passes to the Infantry Battalion Commander and the Blues move back to a PZ for extraction. Employing this procedure over the years, the First Cavalry Division has achieved outstanding results.

7. SECURITY MISSION VERSUS VISUAL RECONNAISSANCE

   a. The true value of Air Cavalry is only realized when it is properly employed. Air Cavalry performs the traditional missions of the cavalry, reconnaissance, security and economy of force. The decision on which one to perform is one that the Air Cavalry commander co-ordinates with the ground commander responsible for the Area of Operations (AO), to determine which mission is the most advantageous for the situation at hand. The final approval to fire into an area, or conduct ground reconnaissance in an area, can only be given by the ground tactical commander, thus the importance of close co-ordination between commanders. This co-ordination is best effected by personal discussions between the two commanders on a daily basis. The Air Cavalry Commander advises the Ground Tactical Commander on the best way to derive maximum benefits from the Air Cavalry.

b. Since Air Cavalry has the inherent ability to conduct reconnaissance throughout their TAOR on a daily basis, they are the one force available to the ground tactical commander which allows him to visually check each part of his AO on a daily basis. The ground tactical commander must not lose sight of the tremendous benefits to be derived by allowing the Air Cavalry Troop to conduct reconnaissance type missions.

c. Security missions are very beneficial to ground units conducting operations in the jungle or in fortified positions. The Pink Team can assist the ground tactical commander by pin-pointing enemy locations, directing the forces around obstacles and by providing early warning. When a ground unit is in a movement to contact, Pink Team coverage should be discouraged. By committing Pink Teams to cover a movement to contact, the ground commander forfeits his reconnaissance capability throughout the remaining portion of his area of operations.

d. As a rule, Air Cavalry operations should be conducted in the far reaches of the TAOR, away from ground operations. This ensures the ground tactical commander total coverage of his assigned area of operations. It is the responsibility of the Air Cavalry Troop commander to advise the ground tactical commander on the best way to employ the troop. Conversely there is little to be gained from reconnaissance if the ground unit is unable to exploit the Air Cavalry Troop findings. Close co-ordination of the total effort is absolutely essential.

8. CROSS ATTACHMENT AND REINFORCEMENT OF AIR CAVALRY TROOPS

It has been the experience of this Air Cavalry Brigade that cross attachment and reinforcement of individual troops is conducted frequently. Cross attachment is defined as attaching teams from one troop to another troop for a period in excess of one day. Reinforcement is simply reinforcing one troop with teams from another troop, or on as required basis, with the commitment to terminate (the support) during the same day. Conditions which require cross attachment or reinforcement are: excessive battle damage, low maintenance availability or Division directed areas of priority. Due to the standard methods of operation in the Air Cavalry Brigade, effecting the cross attachment or reinforcement posed no problems. The Brigade simply called the troops concerned on the radio and directed one troop to provide the designated number of teams or specific type aircraft to another troop. If a particular troop developed maintenance problems or suffered a great deal of battle damage, they initiated the request for reinforcement. The stated objective of the Brigade was to ensure that each troop provided four Pink Teams a day.

When a troop was directed to provide teams to reinforce another troop it was the responsibility of the losing troop commander to inform the ground tactical commander that he would be short the designated number of teams. Due to the stationing of the troops it was possible to reinforce any of the troops within thirty minutes. This capability was not limited to aircraft alone. There were separate occasions when aircraft were shot down in a location far removed from the troop's Blue Platoon. In these situations it was faster to direct a Blue Platoon from another troop to proceed to the scene and secure the downed aircraft and extract the crew. When this occurred the Blue Platoon was placed OPCON to the gaining troop commander until the aircraft and crew were extracted. This underscores and illustrates why it is imperative that the Air Cavalry Troop not be attached or placed OPCON to another maneuver element. On occasion, the Blue Platoon of one troop could be used as the QRF for another troop.

9. RANGER TEAM UTILIZATION

a. During this reporting period H Company 75th Rangers were attached to the Brigade. These Ranger teams provided a wealth of information and invaluable hard intelligence to the overall G2 Division level effort. It was found the Ranger missions and the Air Cavalry missions were entirely compatible and complemented each other. It is felt that within the Air Cavalry Brigade of the future, Ranger companies should be included as a part of the basic organization for combat. A brief discussion on the method of employment follows.

b. Each Ranger team consists of six men. Upon receipt of a mission the team leader prepares his team for the mission. The team leader and assistant team leader are briefed on the area of operations by G2 personnel and then complete a map reconnaissance of the area. The Ranger reconnaissance box is normally 2000 metres by 2000 metres. The team is given two days in which to prepare for insertion. When a primary reconnaissance box is selected, an alternate box must also be selected. When the team leader is on the over flight he conducts reconnaissance of the primary and alternate boxes. The day of their scheduled insertion the team is transported to the friendly unit nearest to the Ranger box. Upon arrival at that location the Ranger Team establishes radio contact with the Ranger Liaison Sergeant, located at the ground tactical commander's headquarters and informs him they are ready for the over flight of the insertion area. The Ranger Team Liaison then informs the Air Cavalry Troop that the team is ready for the over flight and where they can be picked up. An over flight of the area is desirable, as this gives the Team Leader the advantage of actually having seen the terrain over which he will operate. Several methods of over flight were tried, but the best method is to place the Team Leader in the scout aircraft and actually allow him to conduct a low level reconnaissance of the area. Once the over flight is complete the Team Leader rejoins his team and conducts his final briefing. After this briefing is complete, the Ranger Team utilizing Air Cavalry aircraft proceeds low level to the insertion point. The cover aircraft previously used on the over flight gives the lift pilot directions to the Landing Zone (LZ). Utilizing low level flight provides a degree of security and reduces the chance of compromise.

After the insertion is complete, the Ranger Team conducts a communication check with the Ranger Liaison Sergeant at Brigade headquarters. If the team has good communications the lift and cover aircraft are released. If communications are not established the team is extracted and inserted into their alternate box without further clearance from higher headquarters. If the team is unable to establish communication from the alternate box the team is returned to the ground tactical headquarters to replace and recheck the radio equipment or to study another reconnaissance. An inexperienced S2 (Brigade or Battalion level) might well direct a team into a third box without giving the team time to prepare. The Air Cavalry Commander must guard against this. When a Ranger Team is inserted into an area the Air Cavalry Troop responsible for that area provides an overwatch capability. If a team (Ranger) establishes contact and is unable to defeat the enemy, or if the team has been compromised they contact the Ranger Liaison Sergeant who contacts the Air Cavalry Troop. Ranger Teams in contact receive a priority over other missions. A Pink Team is sent to the area and co-ordinates the extraction or provides fire power for the team. If the Ranger Team establishes contact with a large enemy force, the team can be reinforced with the Blues from the Air Cavalry Troop to further develop the situation.

c. Ranger Team insertions must be a totally co-ordinated effort between the Air Cavalry Troop Commander, the Ground Tactical Commander, the Brigade S2 and the Division G2.

10. AUTOMATIC INTELLIGENCE DATA PROCESSING

a. Due to the large area an Air Cavalry Brigade can cover daily there is a tremendous amount of intelligence information that is generated within the Brigade. The present method of storing and recalling this information is totally inadequate. Presently the information is recorded on a card and posted to a map. The entire Division Area of Operations is broken down into 100,000 square metres (boxes). Each of these areas are numbered and have a separate card and map sheet. By faithfully posting all spot reports which include all contacts, ground to air firings, agent reports, Moving Target Indicator (MTI) reports, a picture will soon develop and the enemy will tell us where he is located. This is an invaluable tool and greatly assists the Air Cavalry Commander in determining where to look for the enemy. The big disadvantage to manual postings and recall is the time and manpower required to post and review the information. The amount of information generated by an Air Cavalry Brigade can become unmanageable without some computerization to process, store and recall, on demand, the information that is desired.

    b. The benefits of a tactical computer employed in the intelligence analysis role will only be limited by the imagination of the user. There is no requirement for the computer to be located in the Air Cavalry Brigade headquarters. What would be required would be skilled personnel trained in ADP procedures and a data link to the computer (VHF).

11. AIR CAVALRY UTILIZATION

On several occasions when initial co-ordination was being conducted, the ground commander would ask, "What aviation assets are available to my unit?" Those ground commanders did not realize the value of Air Cavalry operations and they viewed the unit as a source of 3 types of aviation assets to solve their fire power, resupply, and command and control problems. The Air Cavalry Commander must resist every effort of commanders to fragment their unit into an odd job aviation company. The Cavalry commander must explain how the unit is designed to work as a close knit team. Each platoon makes an important contribution to the Cavalry mission and to try to change the procedure reduces the effectiveness of the unit. An Air Cavalry unit is not an aviation unit but rather a reconnaissance maneuver element similar to the armored cavalry. One time exceptions to maintaining troop integrity leads to inconsistency and will worsen rather than help the situation. Direct the ground commander to the proper channel for requesting aviation support and continue with the cavalry mission.

12. REQUIREMENT FOR AN INFANTRY BATTALION IN THE AIR CAVALRY BRIGADE:

There have been numerous occasions when the Brigade could have employed an Infantry Battalion in conjunction with cavalry operations.

Often the ground maneuver battalions were committed to operations that prevented them from exploiting the findings of the Air Cavalry elements. Since the ground maneuver battalions were unable to reinforce, these targets were most often engaged with fire power and there was no ground exploitation. It was also an observation of the Air Cavalry Brigade that the ground maneuver battalions were reluctant to maneuver within 1000 meters of established boundaries. Since the Air Cavalry Troops habitually operated in different battalion AO's throughout the day, the Air Cavalry Troops often exploited this 2000 meter strip between maneuver units. On one occasion during the reporting period the Brigade task organized for a raid mission and had an Infantry battalion placed OPCON to the Brigade. This task organization was very effective and illustrates the possibilities inherent in this type of task organization. Rather than commit the Infantry to ground patrol operations, they were told to exploit what the Air Cavalry located. Certainly one possibility for Air Cavalry Brigade operations in the future is to assign the Brigade a specific area of operations to conduct cavalry operations.

13. AIRCRAFT MAINTENANCE AND SUPPLY PROCEDURES:

a. Maintenance within the Air Cavalry Brigade was probably the most critical area affecting the operations of the Brigade. It is recognized from the onset that the maintenance program of the Air Cavalry Brigade is extremely critical and is as important as the tactical operation. In many cases it is more important. Significant areas related to the maintenance effort of the Brigade will be discussed below.

b. Battle damage. Due to their organic mission, the aircraft of the Brigade experienced an incidence rate of battle damage that can be compared to no other unit. During the period of October 1970 to January 1971, 40 aircraft were damaged by hostile fire. An additional 22 incurred environmental damage ultimately resulting in the turn in of 36 aircraft. However, those aircraft incurring damage and repaired the same day account for many maintenance days. Over 370 aircraft days were lost to unscheduled maintenance during the months of October to December 1970. This does not include the maintenance time lost to recovery, preparation and final turn in of unrepairable aircraft. Turn in procedures need to be simplified and float aircraft established to minimize the aircraft days lost and to allow organic maintenance personnel to concentrate on repairable aircraft.

c. Supply procedures. Technical supply procedures within Vietnam are not in accordance with TM 735-35. Due to local policies, SOP's and other deviations, our few school trained technical supply personnel are at a loss in the modified system. If the doctrinal supply procedures are inadequate, they need to be changed. These changes should be incorporated into the manual and our personnel instructed as to the proper procedures.

d. It is common practice in Infantry, Armor and some Artillery units to conduct periodic stand downs for one or two days. This allows the unit to catch up on these maintenance stand downs, while incurring no further battle damage. Within the Air Cavalry Brigade, the number of Pink Teams required to effectively provide visual reconnaissance remains stable and increases dramatically during periods of enemy activity. Due to the flexibility of Air Cavalry, one troop can adequately cover another troop's AO for one or two days. Each Air Cavalry troop should receive a minimum of one day maintenance stand down per month.

14. EXECUTION

1. Because of the complexities of Air Cavalry operations and the inherent difficulties in presenting the scope of the action in conventional narrative format, the following method of unfolding the action has been chosen.

2. Each significant day will be handled separately, with an accompanying map to illustrate the major movements of the maneuver elements during that period. In cases where the velocity of combat operations increased, enclosures, consisting of diagrams will be provided to better portray the key movements.

3. Additionally, a task organization will be provided for the day that the task organization changes.

15. INTELLIGENCE

1. As of July 1970 the Division has been actively engaged in three basic efforts: locating and destroying enemy caches, interdicting the enemy logistical routes into South Vietnam and eliminating the enemy forces working in the 1st ACD area of operations. Consequently the enemy has continued his efforts to maintain effective logistical routes from Cambodia into Military Region (MR) 3. Basically he has avoided direct fire attacks and used attacks by fire and terrorist activities as his most predominant methods of establishing contact.

2. Friendly elements have been targeted against munitions caches of the 81st Rear Services Group (RSG) in War Zone D. Enemy ammunition stockpiles in War Zone D have been reduced by more than 200 tons of munitions. Through the efforts of the Division, 500 individuals and crew served weapons were discovered in War Zone D during October of 1970. The finds included 2 US 75mm Pack Howitzers. In addition, nearly 4000 grenades and mines were unearthed and 2000 artillery and mortar rounds were discovered.

3. Large rice caches have been discovered in Phuoc Long Province. The largest consisting of 482 tons of polished rice found near the Cambodian border. Indications were that the rice was placed by the 86th RSG for future use by division sized enemy elements upon their return to South Vietnam. Since the American cross-border operation in June 1970, enemy units have been forced to become self-sufficient for rations and clothing.

Lack of food for the enemy has been a critical problem which has resulted in a marked increase of Chieu Hois and ralliers, especially in the 2nd Brigade area of operations.

4. Friendly forces have effectively interdicted infiltration and supply routes into the Division AO, especially in War Zone D. The Serges Jungle highway (Song Be Corridor), the Adams trail and the Jolley road have shown negligible use since July 1970. Friendly operations in Phuoc Long, Binh Long and Western Quang Duc provinces have severely limited the enemy's ability to resupply the

81st RSG from Cambodia. In January 1970 captured documents showed how well friendly elements have countered VC Rear Services activities in MR-7. The 84th RSG disbanded due to its inability to supply units in MR-7. Several elements of the 84th were reassigned to the Rear Services Staff, MR-7, with the rest ordered to return to Cambodia. The Rear Services Staff, MR-7, has assumed the entire function of supply for units in MR-7 and has tailored its procurement elements to employ the Shadow Supply System to the maximum.

5. The H-50 Transportation has been constantly interdicted and its ability to resupply the elements of MR - 6 has been severely limited. Any supplies which it does not infiltrate are forced along a circuitous route which goes well East of the Division's operational boundaries. In addition to blocking the routes followed by the H-50th, supply dumps have been exploited, the most significant of which was found near Fire Support Base (FSB) Snuffy (Bu Gin Map) on 15 December. This cache contained some 17 tons of small arms rounds, mortar, recoilless rifle rounds and fuses and explosives.

6. Thirty pounds of documents captured by Ranger Team #67 on 22 November 1970 after a contact detailed the relationship between the supply procurement units of the 81st RSG and the Shadow Supply System. Revealed were the primary entry and exit points of the Rear Services Group to the East of the LTLIA between Phuoc Vinh and Dong Xoai utilized by the H-2 purchasing units of C11 food procurement Company. It also became apparent that the 81st has sufficient funds for Shadow Supply Operations, as the Rear Services Department of COSVN provides the 81st with large sums of piastres and US 'green backs'.

a. On 3 January, F/2-11 Armored Cavalry Regiment (ACR) detained two individuals, Tran Van Ngan and Le Van Hay, parked in a truck off QL-1 in Long Khanh Province south of FSB Olessen. The truck contained 197, one hundred pound bags of US rice, partially concealed by 40 cases of beer. The supplies had been purchased on the Saigon Black Market for 500,000 piastres and transported to a rendezvous point on QL-1 where the two detainees, while awaiting VC supply personnel to off-load the truck, were arrested. It is significant to note that the truck passed through twelve National Police checkpoints between Saigon and Long Khanh without being detected. Interrogation of Ngan and Hay at ARVN III Corps G2 resulted in the arrest of two other men who acted as VC suppliers for the Rear Services Staff of MR-7. These men are presently being questioned so as to provide extensive information regarding exit and entry points, amounts of supplies and names of suppliers in MR-7.

7. Within the Brigade's Area of Operations the only main force enemy units remaining are the First and Second Battalions and Headquarters of the 33rd NVA Regiment, as well as the C2 Company, 33rd Artillery Battalion. Both the 1st and 2nd Battalions are located in Binh Tuy Province, an area of operations only given to the Brigade on 1 September. Contacts have been made with the 33rd Regiment, but it has refused to stand and fight and has remained relatively untried in combat.

8. Operations within sub-region 5 have been responsible for a breakdown of the once strong Dong Nai Regiment to separate Battalions operating on a much smaller scale than previously. The Dong Nai Regiment disbanded in spring 1970 to assist the District forces of SR-5 in attacking the GVN Pacification Program. Formally comprized of four infantry battalions (K1, K2, K3 and K4) and eight headquarters and support companies, the Regiment underwent drastic reorganization. Personnel of the regimental headquarters were reassigned to SR-5 Headquarters elements or to the battalions. The headquarters support companies were integrated into SR-5 Headquarters, the battalions, or the 'J' series units were subordinated to SR-5 (formally the 500 series). The individual battalions were assigned new areas of operations and were to receive any specific combat missions from the Military Department of SR-5. K1, based in southern Phu Giao District, was designated the mobile reserve battalion of SR-5 to be employed anywhere in SR-5 as a striking force. In actuality, K1's operations will probably be confined to southern Phu Giao, northeastern Chau Thanh and northwestern Tan Uyen Districts. Tan Uyen District Local Force Company is a support force. K3 no longer exists as a unit as all of its personnel were sent to the local forces of the three southern districts of SR-5 (Di An, Lai Thieu and Thu Duc Districts). K4 was assigned to Chau Thanh District to support the C62 Chanh District Local Force Company in disrupting the

GVN Pacification Program.

   a. Friendly elements have had sporadic contacts in Sub-Region 5 since July. The SR-5 Headquarters elements have been contacted periodically. Their present location in southern War Zone D appears much safer for them since friendly pressure forced them to relocate outside the Sub-Region boundary. Joint operations in the Sub-Region have accounted for 504 enemy KIA, 9 PW's, and 22 Chieu Hois.

   b. On 17 September, E/1-9 Cavalry Blues, while conducting ground reconnaissance in the vicinity of YT 052311, south-west of Camp Gorvad, made contact with an estimated platoon size enemy force. The contact resulted in 15 enemy KIA, found to be elements of the K2 Dong Nai Battalion. Continuing allied sweep operations throughout the later part of September continued to disrupt enemy operations, resulting in an additional seven KIA. Throughout September and October, Camp Gorvad was the target of indirect fire attacks. However, on 20 October, while on a visual reconnaissance in the vicinity of YT 062612, E/1-9 Cav spotted and engaged thirteen individuals, found later to be on a food resupply mission. Twelve of these enemy were killed and one was detained. This individual was Khuat Van Ngoc. Under intense interrogation, it was found that Ngoc was a Platoon Leader of C2 Company, K33 Artillery Battalion, and his mission was to periodically attack Camp Gorvad. Upon completion of interrogation, Ngoc was exploited in the field and led Echo Troop to the base area of C2 and C3 companies. Discovered were one 75mm recoilless rifle and one 82mm mortar, which were the weapons used for indirect fire attacks on Camp Gorvad. Since the confiscation of these weapons there has only been one attack by fire on Camp Gorvad, which was attributed to SR-5 elements.

   c. During November and December, activity was light in that portion of the Sub-Region that lies in the Division AO. The disbanded elements of the Dong Nai Regiment have avoided contact. Harassing and terrorist activities are still prevalent but on a much smaller scale than previously. These activities are targeted against the GVN Pacification Program and aim to aid the enemy in proselytizing activities.

9. The only Local Force Battalion remaining in MR-10 is the Song Be Battalion (212 Bn.), as two former battalions, D368 and D168, have been fragmented and assigned to assist the local party structures. In Binh Long Province, the D368 was resubordinated in November 1970 and is known to have one element East of Quan Loi and another Northeast of Loh Ninh. The 168 of Phuoc Long Province has been operating in support of local forces since January 1970. All three battalions have avoided contact with the Division although an element of the D168 may have been responsible for the 12 November indirect fire attack on FSB Buttons.

10. Operations within MR-10 have been concentrated on disrupting the numerous VC production villages in Phuoc Long Province. The success of these efforts can be measured in the crippled control elements of the military region, which has been reduced to such a poor state that it cannot prevent the mass defection of villagers to allied units. Since 21 July there have been 1002 ralliers from VC forced labour villagers in Phuoc Long Province. The VC organization in Phuoc Long Province can only hope to maintain a semblance of administrative control over the dwindling population. A document captured in December revealed that the number of people under MR-10 control has, by Viet Cong documentation, fallen from 30000 to 6000. Since most Viet Cong claims are optimistic, it can be surmized that the situation in MR-10 is indeed desperate for the VC. The figure of 6000 is inflated, as the current estimate of population under VC control is considerably less.

11. Enemy efforts throughout the Brigade AO have shifted in emphasis from attacks on US/ARVN forces to tactics directed toward discrediting the GVN Pacification effort by attacks on PSDF and territorial outposts. The only apparent exception to this policy is found in the border areas, where main force units have engaged ARVN units targeted against the Cambodian base areas.

/s/ Carl M. Putnam
/t/ CARL M. PUTNAM
    LTC   ARMOR
    Commanding

This Map shows the stationing of Air Cavalry Assets from 1 September 1970 through 25 October 1970.

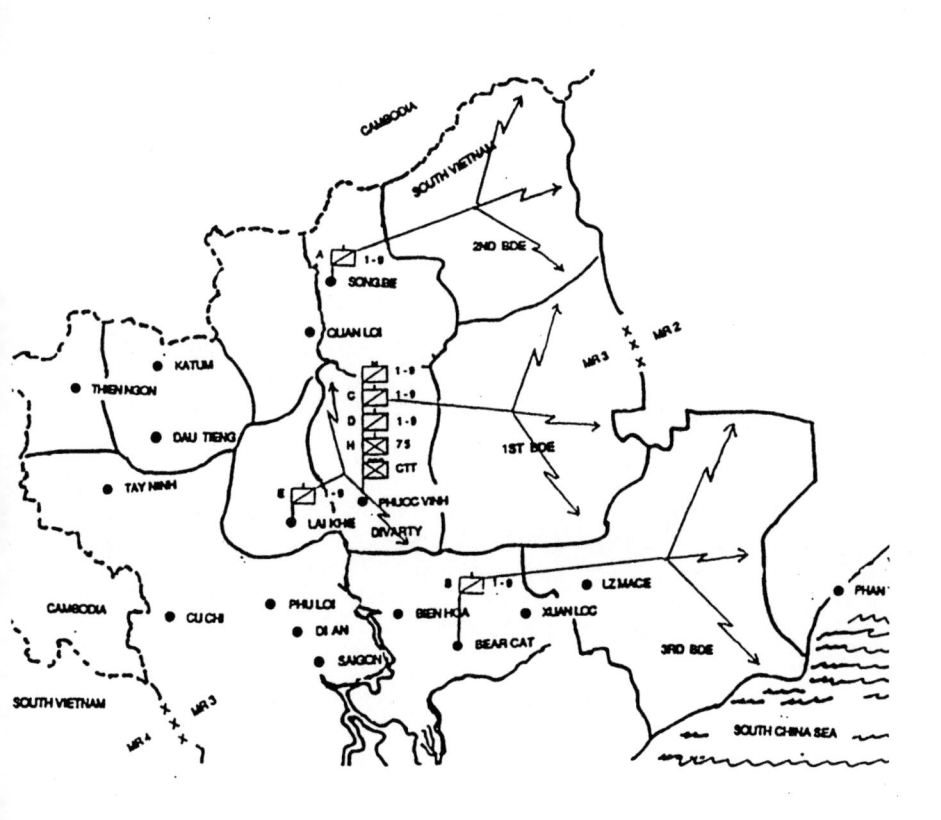

1 September 1970

1. Operations Summary

This day was characterized with light activity and one contact. B/1-9, while conducting a reconnaissance in the vicinity of ZT1 55175 had approximately 30 rounds of small arms fired at a Pink Team. The team engaged the area resulting in 2 NVA killed by helicopter (KBH). E Troop (provisional) was assigned AO Chief as an area of responsibility. This AO was under the tactical control of the DIVARTY Commander. E Troop was also given the mission of providing support for the other troops of the Squadron. This support consisted of releasing OPCON of a designated number of Pink Teams to the Troop Commander, whose AO was designated as requiring reinforcements for that day.

2. Task Organization:

    1-9 ACS
     A/1-9
     B/1-9
     C/1-9
     D/1-9
     E/1-9
     H Co. 75th Rangers (infantry)
     62nd Infantry Platoon, Combat Trackers, (CTT)

3. Intelligence Summary

No change from Division INTSUM.

4. Activities Statistics:

a.
Airmobile Operations	Insertions	Extraction
Ranger Teams	2	3
CTT Teams	0	0
Blues	0	0

b. Aircraft Firings HIT   NOT HIT   CRASHED/DESTROYED
   B Troop   1

c. Friendly Losses   Enemy Losses
   KIA   0   KBH   2
   WIA   0
   MIA   0

2 - 11 September 1970

1. Operations Summary

This ten day period was characterized by scattered contact throughout the Division Area of Operations. The enemy that were located were in small groups of three (3) to five (5) men.

On 2 September 1970, B Troop dispatched a UH-1H to attempt to establish contact with a Ranger Team that had lost communication. The aircraft was presumed down and lost when the troop was unable to establish communication with it. The aircraft was located the following morning with all four crew members KIA.

2. Task Organization

No change

3. Intelligence Summary

On 5 September a patrol received an attack by fire (10X60mm mortar) while entering a cache location of the 81st Rear Services Group, 6 km south of Bunard.

4. Activities Statistics.

a.
Airmobile Operations	Insertions	Extractions
Ranger Teams	15	15
CTT Teams	7	7
Blues	0	0

b.
Aircraft Firings	HIT	NOT HIT	CRASHED/DESTROYED
A Troop		3	
B Troop		2	1
C Troop	2	1	
E Troop	3		

c. Friendly Losses   Enemy Losses
   KIA   4   KBH   26
   WIA   7   KIA   1
   MIA   0   VCS   1
                            VCC   1

12 September 1970

1. Operations Summary

'A' Troop started the day's activities at 0847 hours when a Pink Team observed and engaged 8 NVA at YU501337. This engagement resulted in 2 NVA KBH. To follow up this contact the Blues were inserted at YU501329 at 0953 hours to conduct reconnaissance toward the contact site. At 1055 hours at YU568317 the Pink Team that was covering the Blues observed and engaged 2 VC at YU568317. This engagement resulted in 2 VC KBH.

Further to the South in DIVARTY's AO, E Troop inserted the Blue platoon for general recon. The platoon was inserted at 1055 hours and extracted at 1645 hours with negative significant findings.

At 1550 hours at ZT085316, Bravo Troop Blues were inserted to secure a downed AH-1G that was supporting the Troop. This aircraft was from E Troop and had an engine failure while performing VR. At 1745 the aircraft was recovered and at 1750 hours the Blues were extracted.

At 1620 hours the C Troop Blues were inserted at YT175495 to secure a CH-47 that had gone down in that general vicinity. The Blues were extracted at 1730 hours.

At 1645 hours Alpha Troop Blues captured a VC who stated there were 150 more VC located 200 metres west of their location. The Pink Team working over the Blues conducted reconnaissance of this area and observed several VC, engaged the area, resulting in 3 VC KBH. While this action was taking place, another Pink Team of Alpha Troop observed 50 - 100 individuals and immediately engaged this force. While making repeated passes over the enemy positions the Pink Team became the target for intense ground to air fire. At this time the team leader requested a section of AFA and an airstrike. Alpha Troop and AFA continued to work this area until 1930 hours. Results of this were 13 VC KBH and 3 NVA KBH for Alpha Troop and 2 VC KBAFA. At 1900 hours Alpha Troop Blues were extracted.

At 2345 hours the Squadron Headquarters area became the target of a direct fire attack by a 75mm Recoilless Rifle, six (6) rounds impacted at 2345, with another three (3) rounds impacting at 0014 hours, 13 September 1970. This attack resulted in 5 U.S. WIA, one building destroyed, and one UH-1H sustaining moderate damage.

2. Task Organization:

No change

3. Intelligence Summary:

During the preceding four (4) days it became apparent that the enemy was making an effort to infiltrate across the border into the 2nd Bde AO. There was also evidence that the enemy was attempting to gather rice from the Rice Bowl in the 3rd Bde AO. Both of these areas were Division Areas of Interest. The Squadron reinforced A & B Troop by providing two (2) teams for each troop from E Troop.

4. Activities Statistics:

a. Airmobile Operations	Insertions	Extractions
Ranger Teams	0	0
CTT Teams	1	1
Blues	5	5

b. Aircraft Firings	HIT	NOT HIT	CRASHED/DESTROYED
A Troop		4	

c. Friendly Losses		Enemy Losses	
KIA	0	KBH	23
WIA	5	KIA	0
MIA	0	VCC	1
		KBAFA	1

13-16 September 1970

1. Operations Summary

This four day period was characterized with light scattered contact throughout the Division AO. The most significant contact occurred on 16 September at YU551274 at 0810 hours when Ranger Team 72 engaged ten (10) NVA approaching their position. This contact was brief and devastating, resulting in six (6) NVA KIA. The contact broke at 0812 hours.

Throughout this period E Troop reinforced A & B Troop by assigning two (2) teams to work directly for each of these troops. Emphasis was placed along the border in Alpha Troop's AO and around the Rice Bowl in B Troop's AO.

2. Task Organization:

No change

3. Intelligence Summary:

Continued surveillance on the Adams Trail and the Jolly Trail at their border crossing points denied the enemy access to his caches in North Phouc Long Province.

4. Activities Statistics:

a.
Airmobile Operations	Insertions	Extractions
Ranger Teams	0	0
CTT Teams	6	6
Blues	0	0

b.
Aircraft Firings	HIT	NOT HIT	CRASHED/DESTROYED
A Troop	2	1	
C Troop	1		

c. Friendly Losses   Enemy Losses
    KIA   0   KBH   3
    WIA   1   KIA   6
    MIA   0   VCC   1
                             VCS   2
                             KBAFA   0

17 September 1970

1. Operations Summary:

On this date E Troop was the first troop to make contact. At 0905 hours the Troop Commander was performing reconnaissance to locate a suitable LZ to put the Blues into, when 2 NVA were observed at YT049315 hiding in a bomb crater. The Troop Commander and his cover ship engaged the area, resulting in 2 NVA KBH. An LZ was selected nearby and the Blues inserted at 1002 hours. At 1040 hours the Pink Team over the Blues observed and engaged another individual resulting in one VC KBH. The Blues were working towards the original contact site when they moved into a bunker complex. On checking out the first bunker they came upon numerous medical supplies and a heavy blood trail. The Platoon Leader directed one squad to follow the blood trail for a short distance and establish security for the platoon. At 1140 this element established contact with an unknown size enemy force. The QRF was called for and inserted, followed shortly by the RRF. This was considered a classic example of Air Cavalry Operations and resulted in a First Team Combat Action Report being prepared. This report is contained in enclosure 1.[*]

At 1055 hours a Pink Team from B Troop was conducting reconnaissance when the White Bird received heavy .30 calibre machine gun fire, resulting in an unknown number of hits. The aircraft lost power and crashed resulting in the three crewmen being WIA. B Troop Blues were inserted at 1120 hours to secure the aircraft and extract the crew. At 1430 hours the Blues were extracted.

At 1650 hours Alpha Troop observed one (1) NVA at YU301510. They engaged, resulting in 1 NVA KBH.

2. Task Organization:

No change

---

[*] EDITORIAL NOTE: The First Team Combat Action Report follows this day's activities.

3. Intelligence Summary.

Documents captured by E/1-9 Blues identified the medical staff of Tan Uyen District.

4. Activities Statistics:

a. | Airmobile Operations | Insertions | Extractions |
   | --- | --- | --- |
   | Ranger Teams | 0 | 0 |
   | CTT Teams | 0 | 0 |
   | Blues | 2 | 2 |

b. | Aircraft Firings | HIT | NOT HIT | CRASHED/DESTROYED |
   | --- | --- | --- | --- |
   | B Troop | | | 1 |
   | E Troop | | 1 | |

c. Friendly Losses   Enemy Losses
    KIA 0   KBH 4
    WIA 4   KIA 5
    MIA 0   VCC 0
                      VCS 0
                      KBAFA 0

DEPARTMENT OF THE ARMY
HEADQUARTERS, 1ST CAVALRY DIVISION
(AIRMOBILE)
APO SAN FRANCISCO 96490

AVDAGT-DT   5 October 1970

FIRST TEAM COMBAT
ACTION REPORT NR3

AIR CAVALRY OPERATION

Contained herein is an example of a successfully executed Air Cavalry operation by the Blues of E/1-9 Cav, 1/A/1-12 Cav (QRF), and C/1-12 Cav (RRF) with OPCON 1/B/1-12 Cav.

1. GENERAL SITUATION. On 17 September 1970, 1-12 Cav was conducting ground reconnaissance and ambush operations in areas north, north-east, east, and west of Camp Gorvad. These operations were designed to interdict movement of enemy personnel and equipment in the area and preempt enemy plans to attack Camp Gorvad by fire during the 18 September high point. At 0905 hours, at YT049305, a low bird from E/1-9 Cav spotted and engaged two individuals resulting in two enemy killed by helicopter. Recent trail activity in this area was also noted by the hunter-killer team.

2. INSERTION OF BLUES (E/1-9 Cav). To develop the situation the CO, E/1-9 recommended the insertion of the Blues which was approved by CO, 1-12 Cav. The Blues were inserted into YT054295 at 1002 hours by the E Troop Commander. Their mission was to conduct ground reconnaissance operations west into the tree line to gain contact with enemy troops suspected of being in the area. At 1040 hours, the hunter-killer team spotted and engaged one enemy soldier 100 meters north of the LZ resulting in one KBH. At 1120 hours, the platoon discovered a bunker complex 400 meters west of the LZ. Shortly thereafter (1140 hrs) they made contact with an estimated enemy platoon in the complex. The enemy was engaged with organics

and ARA, with the Blues receiving SA and AW fire in return. The results were five enemy KIA and one KCS WIA. At 1200 hours, the Blues moved back to the LZ to medevac the wounded trooper.

    3. INSERTION OF 1/A/1-12 Cav (QRF). To reinforce the Blues, the Battalion QRF (1/A/1-12 Cav) was inserted into the same LZ at 1232 hours by the E Troop Commander. Following link-up, the Platoon Leaders quickly exchanged information after which the Platoon Leader of 1/A/1-12 Cav and nine men moved forward to the bunker complex. The E Troop Commander remained in command of both ground units which regained contact at 1315 hours and killed five enemy soldiers with no friendly casualties. They also discovered six bunkers 5' X 10' and two command and control bunkers 10' X 20' with three spider holes for exits. The bunkers which were made of corrugated steel, and sandbags contained: 35 pounds of medical supplies; seven pounds of documents, 35 CHICOM grenades, and 15 U.S. Frag grenades. The QRF and the Blues collectively captured three AK-47's and two M-16 rifles. The QRF Platoon Leader estimated a 50-60 man element had at one time occupied the bunker complex.

    4. INSERTION OF C/1-12 Cav (RRF). Based on the foregoing, the decision was made to employ a company size force in the area. The First Platoon of C Company was inserted at 1420 hours, and moved immediately to the contact area. The Battalion Commander, 1-12 Cav took command of the ground units when the RRF was inserted. After securing the area the RRF drove further into the bunker complex. The Blues and 1/A/1-12 Cav (QRF) were extracted at 1710 hours. At 1800 hours, contact with the enemy was re-established resulting in two enemy troops killed, with no U.S. casualties. Simultaneously, 1/B/1-12 Cav was air assaulted into YT408309 and established blocking positions along suspected avenues of egress north-west of the contact area. Success for FIRST TEAM elements continued the following day as C Company made a ground reconnaissance of the general area. At 1015 hours, near YU052311, a bunker was located which contained 1 AK-47 bandoleer, 2 AK-47 magazines, 90 rounds of AK-47 ammunition, 1 U.S. 60 mm mortar round, 3 B-40 rounds, 1 M-28 U.S. gas mask, and seven blasting caps. A second bunker containing 1 old B-40 round was located at

1030 hours vicinity YT052297. A thorough search of this area resulted in the capture of a wounded enemy soldier at 1310 hours.

5. SUMMARY AND LESSONS LEARNED.

   a. Summary. This operation resulted in 15 enemy KIA, 1 enemy POW, with 1 KCS (Kit Carson Scout) WIA. This tactical success is attributed to several fundamental airmobile tactics and techniques which were successfully implemented by the Infantry, Air Cavalry, Artillery, and aviation units.

   (1) The units quickly combined their resources to maintain momentum and contact, and keep the enemy off balance.

   (2) Command and control was clear-cut at all times and changed hands smoothly.

   (3) Both the QRF and the RRF quickly moved to the contact area after respective insertions; thereby maintaining the impetus of the attack.

   (4) The artillery provided timely and effective blocking fires and employed ARA in support of ground troops throughout the day. Included in this support was tube artillery fires from outside the Division AO.

   (5) Lift assets responded promptly thereby enabling the ground commander to maneuver his forces into and out of the contact area.

   (6) The co-ordination and flexibility demonstrated by commanders and their respective staffs contributed to the basic framework for the operation; however, aggressiveness, teamwork and the mission-oriented attitude of the infantrymen, firing batteries, and aircraft crews during the execution phase made the operation a success.

b. Lessons Learned.

(1) Rapid exploitation of a developing enemy Situation is a characteristic of airmobility and should be a matter of SOP in all combat units.

(2) Continued pressure on the enemy, once he is located, prevents him from effectively reconstituting his defenses.

(3) Effective co-ordination between withdrawing and reinforcing infantry elements, to include ground guides, assists in maintaining the initiative in the contact area.

(4) Multi-ship LZ's should be selected during the 'Pile-On' operations to permit the commitment of maximum troops to reinforce at any given time.

(5) Known or suspected enemy weaknesses should be exploited immediately. There were early indications that the bunker complex was a medical facility; therefore it was assumed that the enemy force consisted of rear service elements and not main force groups. Aggressive action by friendly forces against an inferior force provided the key to this tactical success.

(6) The teamwork exhibited by the air cavalry troop commander and the infantry battalion commander in controlling this operation is the hallmark of a successful airmobile operation.

2 Incl /s/ Roderic E. Ordway
1. Sequence of events /t/ RODERIC E. ORDWAY
2. Diagram of contact area LTC, GS
ACofS, G3

DISTRIBUTION:
A Plus
100 - G3 D&T
2 - USARV, J3 DST
2 - IIFFV G3 FDT

SEQUENCE OF EVENTS

TIME	EVENT	RESULTS
0920 17 Sep 70	Pink Team engaged 2 enemy	2 enemy KBH
1002	Blues inserted	
1040	Pink Team engaged 1 enemy	1 enemy KBH
1120	Blues discover bunker complex contact made with estimated enemy platoon.	5 enemy KIA 1 KCS WIA Cptr: 1 AK-47, 2 M-16
1200	Blues move back to LZ	
1232	1/A/1-12 Cav (QRF) inserted into LZ.	
1315	QRF in contact in bunker complex	5 enemy KIA. Cptr: 2 AK-47's, 35 lbs medical supplies, 7 lbs documents, 35 Chicom grenades, 15 U.S. frag grenades.
1335	Contact broken	
1420	C/1-12 Cav (RRF) inserted	
1710	Blues and 1/A/1-12 Cav were extracted.	
1800	C/1-12 Cav in contact in the bunker complex.	2 enemy KIA

1800	1/B/1-12 Cav combat assaulted into blocking position.	
1015 18 Sep 70	C/1-12 Cav located bunker complex	Cptr: 1 AK-47 bandoleer, 2 AK-47 magazines, 90 rds AK-47 ammunition, 1 US 60mm mortar rd, 3 B-40 rds, 1 M-28 gas mask, 7 blasting caps.
1310	C/1-12 Cav located one enemy wounded soldier.	1 enemy POW

Diagram of Contact Area

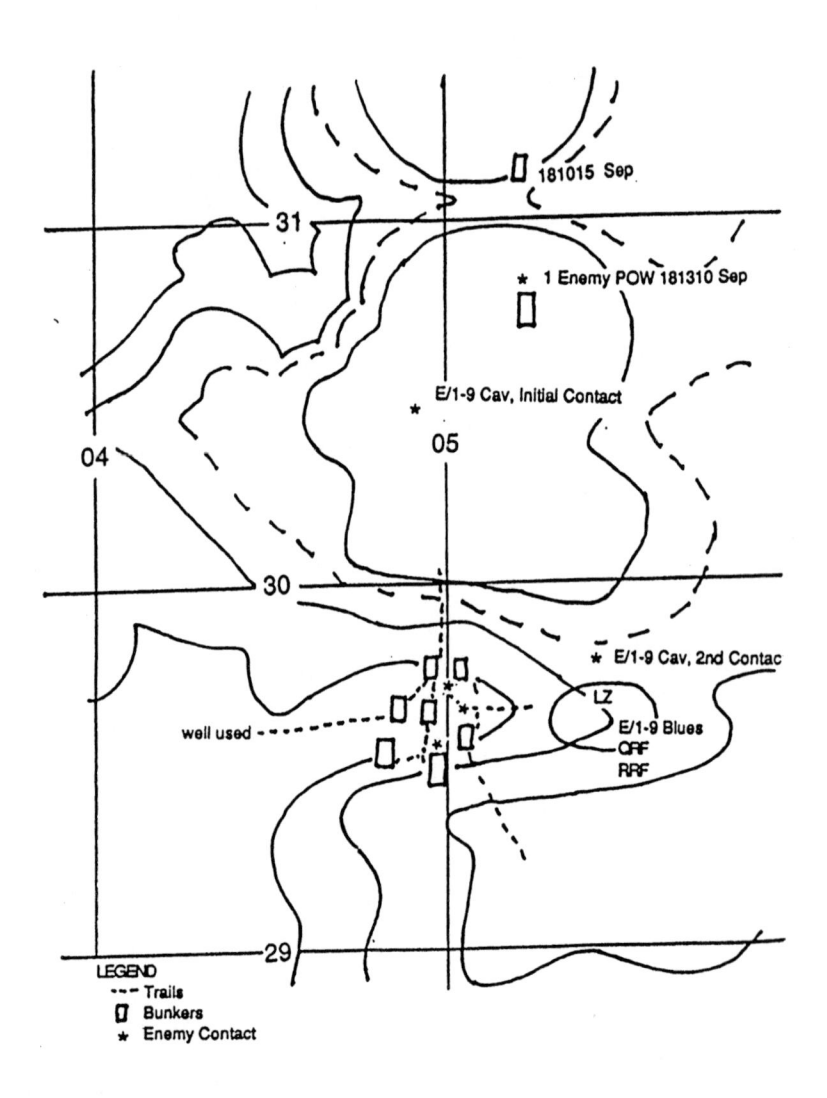

181015 Sep

1 Enemy POW 181310 Sep

E/1-9 Cav, Initial Contact

E/1-9 Cav, 2nd Contac

LZ

E/1-9 Blues
CRF
RRF

well used

LEGEND
- - - Trails
▯ Bunkers
★ Enemy Contact

18 - 30 September 1970

1. Operations Summary

The remaining 13 days of this month were characterized with scattered contact throughout the Division AO. The Squadron continued to place emphasis along the border and Rice Bowl Area. These scattered contacts were typical of the far ranging Air Cavalry operations. Usually these operations were in the far reaches of the AO, away from friendly units.

On the 19th and 25th of the month, Camp Gorvad received harassing mortar and rocket attacks from the K-33 Artillery Battalion. These attacks were of short duration and consisted of six (6) to ten (10) rounds on each occasion.

2. Task Organization:

No change

3. Intelligence Summary.

The attacks by fire, by K-33 Arty Bn., indicate the enemy's interest in limited offensive actions only.

4. Activities Statistics

a. | Airmobile Operations | Insertions | Extractions |
| --- | --- | --- |
| Ranger Teams | 26 | 30 |
| CTT Teams | 13 | 13 |
| Blues | 13 | 13 |

b. | Aircraft Firings | HIT | NOT HIT | CRASHED/DESTROYED |
| --- | --- | --- | --- |
| A Troop | 1 | 2 | |
| B Troop | 5 | 2 | 1 |
| C Troop | 1 | 1 | |
| E Troop | | 4 | 1 |
| HHT | | 1 | |

c. Friendly Losses   Enemy Losses

KIA	2	KBH	51
WIA	5	KIA	5
MIA	0	VCS	14
		KBAFA	2
		KBARTY	9
		KBAS	5

A comparison of the statistics for the 1st Cav Div is reflected below. This comparison reflects the percentage of kills for the 1st Sqdn, 9th Cav in contrast to the rest of the Division.

	AUGUST	SEPTEMBER
Division Total	197	232
1-9 Total	80	126
1-9 Initiated Kills	114	150
1-9 Percent of Division Total	34	54
1-9 Percent of Initiated Kills	58	65

The comparison between the month of August and September illustrates how one additional Air Cavalry Troop affected the results achieved. During the months of June, July, and August the Squadron had maintained an average of 30% of the Division kills. With the addition of E Troop the total percentage jumped to 54%. It is also significant to mention that during the month, the Squadron initiated 65% of all actions that resulted in kills for the division.

The results achieved with the addition of another Air Cav Troop were not unexpected. The additional terrain that came under surveillance increased the probability that more enemy would be detected.

A recapitulation of the Activities Statistics for the month is as follows:

Friendly Losses		Enemy Losses	
KIA	6	KBH	109
WIA	22	KIA	17
MIA	0	WIA	1
		VCS	17
		VCC	4
		KBAFA	4
		KBARTY	9
		KBAS	5

* Authors Note: While LTC Putnam made a valid assumption; "The additional terrain that came under surveillance increased the probability that more enemy would be detected." However, there was not a corresponding increase in results with the addition of other provisional Air Cavalry Troops. LTC Putnam addresses this on page two of the Combat After Action report when he states, "Subsequent Air Cavalry Troops were formed within the Brigade but E Troop met with singular success primarily because of the Armor and Air Cavalry experience of the Troop Commander." MAJ Hilbert H. Chole (the author of this publication) was the Commander of E Troop at its formation and offers these comments:

"Having served in B Troop in 1967 as the Scout Platoon Leader and Troop Operations Officer and then moved to the Squadron Headquarters as the S2 and the S3 during the last month of 1967 and the first six months of 1968 I knew Air Cavalry Operations. In addition to Air Cavalry operations in an Airmobile Division, I knew the Division SOP on Airmobile operations and had participated in hundreds of them from the Bong Son plains through the relief of Khe San and the incursion into the Ashu Valley. I had one year of front line Air Cavalry experience under my belt when I arrived to form E Troop. But in addition to my personal experience, I was blessed to have had some real warriors assigned to E Troop. They were the "Black Sheep" of the Squadron when they were assigned to the troop, but did they love a fight (not all of which was in the AO). All I had to do was show them how I wanted it done, then get out of their way."

1 - 19 October 1970

   1. Operations Summary

   During this period the Squadron had contact with the enemy 19 days out of 19. The ability to find and fight the enemy in small groups of 2 to 5 individuals is characteristic of this phase of operations. This type of recon, tracking and locating small groups of dismounted troops, is without a doubt, the most difficult type of reconnaissance Air Cavalry can be called upon to perform.
   On the 5th and 11th of October Phouc Vinh was the target of indirect fire attacks consisting of mortar and rockets.
   A typical day's operations during this period is as follows:

   14 October 1970

   0745   B Troop scout (OH-6A) received small arms fire. Engaged area with organics with undetermined result.

   0835   B Troop Blues inserted to check out area where scout took fire.

   0900   B Troop Blues extracted with negative significant findings.

   1027   A Troop inserted the Blues for general reconnaissance. Insertion prompted by recent trail activities.

   1115   B Troop Blues inserted for ground recon to check out area that showed movement yesterday.

   1150   B Troop Blues extracted with negative significant findings.

   1210   Ranger Team 55 extracted.

   1425   Ranger Team 51 extracted.

   1516   A Troop Blues extracted with negative significant findings.

   1520   A Troop Blues reinserted to check out bunker complex.

1525   E Troop Blues inserted to check out recent trail activity.

1535   Ranger Team 52 extracted.

1557   Ranger Team 56 inserted.

1605   Ranger Team 72 inserted.

1626   A Troop Pink Team covering the Blues observed and engaged 5 NVA attempting to evade contact with the Blues. This resulted in 2 NVA KBH, with the remaining 3 evading into the jungle.

1630   Ranger Team 76 observed 3 NVA 200 meters west of their location and adjusted artillery fire into the area with unknown results.

1725   E Troop Blues moved into a bunker complex and established contact with an unknown size enemy unit. This contact resulted in one (1) friendly KIA and one (1) friendly WIA.

1745   E Troop Blues broke contact.

1818   A Troop Blues extracted with negative significant finding.

1820   Ranger Team 75 extracted.

2000   E Troop Blues reinforced by QRF and will remain in overnight.

This extract of the Daily Journal for this particular day illustrates how the Squadron continually sought the enemy through the combination of visual reconnaissance and ground reconnaissance conducted by the Blue Platoons and Ranger Teams.

2. Task Organization:

No Change

3. Intelligence Summary.

No Change

4. Activities Statistics:

a. Airmobile Operations   Insertions   Extractions

	Insertions	Extractions
Ranger Teams	32	33
CTT Teams	15	15
Blues	42	42

b. Aircraft Firings

	HIT	NOT HIT	CRASHED/DESTROYED
A Troop	2	10	
B Troop	1	7	
C Troop	4	10	2
E Troop	5	8	2

c. Friendly Losses
Friendly		Enemy	
KIA	4	KBH	75
WIA	21	KIA	12
MIA	1	WIA	1
		VCS	0
		VCC	0
		KBAFA	6
		KBARTY	0
		KBAS	1

20 October 1970

1. Operations Summary.

This day started as a routine day, typical of the scattered contacts we were experiencing throughout this period. At 0915 hours at YT376656 a Pink Team from C Troop received 20 rounds of small arms fire which resulted in negative hits or injuries to the crew. They immediately engaged the area with organics and requested artillery and an air strike to be placed in the area. As this contact developed, the Troop recorded a total of three additional aircraft firings throughout the day, resulting in one AH-1 G from AFA being shot down at 0935 hours. C Troop inserted their Blues to secure the aircraft at 0955 at YT364655. At 1207 hours the aircraft had been recovered and the Blues extracted. Results of this contact were five (5) NVA KBH. At 1430 hours at YT181427 C Troop observed two (2) NVA evade into a bunker. They engaged the bunker, resulting in two (2) NVA KBH.

At 1250 hours E Troop observed and engaged 10 NVA located at YT059615. The Pink Team placed a heavy volume of fire at point blank range, resulting in 9 NVA KBH. This team attempted to locate the other individual but was unsuccessful. The only LZ in the area was a single ship hover down. The decision was made by the Troop Commander to use the LZ and the first ship with Blues was inserted at 1410 hours. On lift out from the LZ the Crew Chief on this aircraft observed 1 NVA in a tree on the LZ. The Crew Chief engaged this individual and shot off the limb the NVA was sitting on. The NVA fell to the ground and immediately surrendered to the Blues. This NVA soldier turned out to be a Warrant Officer from C-2 of the K-33 Arty Bn. of the NVA 64th Arty. He proved to be very co-operative, later leading the Blues to hidden weapons located in the DIVARTY AO (later in the month).*

After the rest of the Blues were inserted, they moved to the contact site and discovered two (2) more NVA soldiers killed by the helicopter. While sweeping the area the Blues engaged two (2)

---

* The final interrogation report on this POW follows this day's activities.

additional NVA who attempted to evade, resulting in 2 NVA KIA.

At 1700 hours B Troop Blues were inserted to conduct ground reconnaissance in an area that showed recent use. At 1800 hours the Blues were extracted with negative significant findings.

2. Task Organization:

No change

3. Intelligence Summary:

The identification of the K-33 Army Bn. and the POW proved valuable by revealing the location of its cache of 1 X 75mm RR and 1 X 82mm mortar.

4. Activities Statistics:

a. Airmobile Operations Insertions Extractions
   Ranger Teams   0   0
   CTT Teams   2   2
   Blues   3   3

b. Aircraft Firings HIT NOT HIT CRASHED/DESTROYED
   C Troop   4

c. Friendly Losses   Enemy Losses
   KIA   0   KBH   12
   WIA   0   KIA   2
   MIA   0   WIA   0
                        VCS   0
                        NVAC   0
                        KBAFA   3
                        KBARTY   0
                        KBAS   0

FINAL INTERROGATION REPORT   022100 November 1970

a. REPORT NUMBER: 407-4

b. NAME: Khuat Van Ngoc (KHUAATS VEAN NGOCV)

c. RANK/POSITION/CATEGORY: WO/Plat Leader-NVA/HC

d. UNIT: B-1 Platoon, C-2 Company, K-3 (AKA K-33) Battalion, F-64 Regiment, 75th Division.

e. DATE AND PLACE OF CAPTURE: 201400 Oct 1970, at YT062612

f. CAPTURING UNIT: E/1-9

g. DISPOSITION: Camp Gorvad, RVN

h. DATE AND PLACE OF BIRTH: 1940 at Hach Loch (V), Phuc Tho (D), Son Tay (P), NVN.

i. EDUCATION: 7 yrs.

j. CIVILIAN OCCUPATION: Farmer

k. DATE OF INDUCTION: Jan 1966, at Ha Tay (P), NVN.

1. TRAINING DATA: Ngoc stated that he received 5 months training with the 1st Mortar Battalion. This training consisted of infantry, artillery and CBR instruction. In Apr 1966, the 1st Mortar Bn. moved to Quang Binh (P), NVN to train. In Jul 1966, the 1st Mortar Bn. became known as the My Tho Group and prepared to infiltrate.

m. INFILTRATION DATA: The My Tho Group, numbering approximately 600 men, began infiltrating in Jul 1966. In Oct 1966, the group arrived in the area of Gia Lai (B-3), SVN. The group renamed the K-33 Mortar Battalion under the E-40 Regiment. In Oct 1967, the K-33 Bn. separated from the 40th Regiment and moved to

Tay Ninh (SVN) where it became subordinate to a newly formed Mortar Regiment, the F-64 (formerly known as E-96). At this time, K-33 Bn. became known as K-3 Bn.

n. LETTER BOX NUMBERS, ALSO KNOWN AS CODE NUMBERS: The LBN for K-3 is 91810 YK.

o. MISSION:

(1) SOURCE'S MISSION AT TIME OF CAPTURE (TOC): At TOC, Ngoc and his platoon were returning from a mission of collecting flour from a cache near the Man Tung (stream) area. The flour approx. 200 kg, was placed there by an element of the 81st RSG. The Hoi Chanh stated that this was the only food supply mission that he ever went on. Other platoons have returned to the C-2 base area with rice, corn and flour.

(2) UNITS MISSION AT TIME OF CAPTURE: The C-2 Mortar Company had been given a general mission - to periodically mortar Camp Gorvad. On DOC, the company was continuing this mission (although it was not actively engaged at the precise time of capture).

(3) SOURCE'S PAST MISSION: As a Platoon Leader, Ngoc was actively engaged in recent missions around the Phouc Vinh area.

(4) UNITS PAST MISSION: Since 1 June 1970, the B-1 platoon has participated in mortaring Camp Gorvad 3 times. Ngoc was not absolutely positive regarding the dates on which these missions were performed, but he gave the following: 17 June 1970, 12 Aug 1970, and 11-12 Oct 1970. B-1 was sent to fire DK-75 rounds into Phouc Vinh. At this time, B-1 fired 9 DK-75mm rounds at Camp Gorvad. The DK-75 was buried in vic XT 9751 and the unit moved to Man Tung (exact location unknown) about 8 km east of Bunard City Post (in Phouc Long) to get food. On returning the unit was ambushed at YT062612.

Ngoc stated that most likely the B-1 and B-2 Platoons of C-2 had been engaged in similar missions during this time; he was, however, unable to furnish any positive information regarding the actions of these units.

On 11 - 12 Oct 1970, the fire point for the B-1 Platoon was in the vic XT 978536.

(5) UNITS FUTURE MISSION: Ngoc stated that as far as he knew, the mission of C-2 would continue to be to continue harassing Camp Gorvad. He had heard that C-2 had received orders to mortar Camp Gorvad 3 times in October 1970 and three times in November 1970.

p. ORGANIZATION AND STRENGTH: The F-64 Regiment (formerly E-96) is subordinate to the 75th Division (F-75) (formerly 69th Division). The K-3 Battalion (formerly the K-33) AKA K-3, is subordinate to F-64. K-3 is composed of three mortar companies, designated C-1, C-2, C-3 (there are over 200 men in the battalion). K-3 is also composed of a HQ section, one rear service team, one recon pit and one communications platoon. C-1 company (AKA ?) is composed of approximately 100 men divided into three platoons, designated as B-1, B-2, B-3, (each platoon has two squads consistently designated as A-1 and A-2). C-2 Company (AKA V-4) is composed of approximately 47 men. Ngoc stated C-2 was more autonomous than either C-1 or C-3, yet all three companies received orders from K-3. The C-3 company (AKA V-6) is composed of approximately 50 - 60 men. C-2 and C-3 are structurally composed exactly as is C-1.

q. WEAPONS AND EQUIPMENT:

NO.		RDS/WPN
	C-1	
1	Rocket Launcher	
2	H-12 Rockets	
2	82mm Mortar	
	C-2	
1	82mm Mortar	?
1	DK-75 (organic to C-2)	?
1	B-41	5
1	B-40	5
28	AK-47s	120

1   15 - watt radio (to contact K-3)

   B-l, C-2
5   AK-47s
1   B-40   5
1   B-41   5

   C-3
1   DK - 75mm
1   82mm Mortar
1   62mm Mortar
?   122 Rockets

  r. LOSSES AND REPLACEMENTS: Since June 70, C-2 has lost no men (except for the recent ambush). In Mar 70, C-2 received 12 new men, and in Sep 70, the unit got 5 new men.

  s. LOGISTICS: C-2 Company received food and weapons from 81st RSG. The food was usually picked up at a point designated by the 81st RSG (as described in sub-paragraph 1 of paragraph o, above).

  The 81st RSG also supplied C-2 with weapons. Members of C-2 would go to a cache site of the 81st. Ngoc stated the location of this cache was in the vic. of XT9868 (this site is near Man Tung.[3]) Ngoc stated that he had been to this area several times in 1969. The cache site was supposedly heavily mined; therefore messengers would wait on the outer perimeter of the area to receive supplies. In 1969, American troops made contact in this area (hearsay). Also Ngoc had heard that on 13 - 14 Oct 70, American troops were in this area. Ngoc believes however, that even if the Allies were in the area, they would not be able to find the weapons/food cache because the cache(s) were buried deeply underground (hearsay). Ngoc stated that he had never been allowed inside the perimeter of the area. The last contact that C-2 had made with 81st RSG (for weapon resupply) was in 1969, when C-2 received DK-75mm rounds, 82mm mortar rounds and H-12 rockets. The 3 platoons of C-2 would requisition supplies for the company (ammo). The C-2 Company also buried its weapons. Ngoc

---

[3] AUTHOR'S NOTE: The interrogator could not locate Man Tung on the map at hand.

did not know the location of the C-2 cache, but he supposed it to be near the C-2 area. He knew that this cache contained an undetermined amount of 82mm mortar rounds, 75mm rounds and possibly 122 rockets. Personnel from the platoon who had been sent for supplies were kept waiting on the perimeter of the cache site until the orders were filled. C-2 personnel would bring the ammo to the messengers.

t. AREA OF OPERATIONS: Since early 1969, C-2 has relocated 3 times. Previously, C-2 was in an area which was possibly west of Suoi Nhung Stream (one had to cross this stream to go to Man Tung).

Since 12 August 1970 C-2 has been operating in an area roughly bordered by these co-ordinates: XT978665, XT988665 (east-west), and XT984672, XT 984662 (north-south).

u. BASE AREA: At the time of the last interrogation (1 Nov 1970), Ngoc had already led allied troops to the former base area of C-2 and C-3. C-2 vic. XT983664, C-3 vic. YT140620.

Ngoc further located K-3 Bn. HQ at YT120610, however, this site was current as of May 1970. In May 1970, K-3 moved to Binh Long (P), but Ngoc could offer no more positive information as to the present location of K-3. In May 1969, C-1 was located in vic. YT140590, but the unit moved to Binh Long in Jul 1969 and was to mortar the 'TECNIT' base at Quan Loi. In Sep 1970, C-3 moved to Bu Dop while C-2 was left in the Phouc Vinh area. Before C-3 departed it left 1 X 82mm Mortar with C-2.

v. TACTICS:

(1) METHOD OF MOVEMENT: When C-2 would relocate, the unit would march during the day in the jungle and occasionally making use of roads at night. The soldiers marched in single file with the lead elements consisting of men armed with AK's and at least one B-40. If the unit were caught in an ambush, it was to retreat. If fire was extremely heavy, the B-40 would be used, but if fire was light, the weapon would be evacuated.

(2) METHODS OF AMBUSH: Ngoc stated that his mortar

company did not engage in any ambushes of Allied Troops. There are no Sapper elements attached to K-3.

(3) METHOD OF PRE-ATTACK: Usually the orders for a mission were received 8 - 10 hours prior to departure. During this time the men would check out the equipment and plan firing sites. The new men in C-2 were given OJT. In the last mission (11 Oct 1970) Ngoc himself showed a new man how to operate the DK-75. The new replacements came to C-2 trained as infantry men (all replacements came to C-2 trained as Infantry and are, recently, NVA).

(4) EVASIVE TACTICS: Ngoc stated that while en route, C-2 would make every effort to evade contact with Allied forces. Scouting patrols would constantly bring back reports of enemy locations. If the C-2 base area was attacked the company would try to defend it, otherwise C-2 would avoid all contact. Ngoc said, however, that no unified plan of retreat had ever been issued.

w. PERSONALITIES:

75TH DIVISION

| CO | Ba Vu (BA VU) | COL 35 yrs (approx) |
| PO | San Tong (SAUS TONGL) | COL 38 yrs (approx) |

F-64 REGIMENT

CO	Lai (LAI)	Lt. Col 42 yrs
XO	Lat (LAAT)	Lt. Col 41 yrs
PO	Lien (LIEEN)	Major 37 yrs
OOFS	Cui (CUIS)	

K-3 Battalion

CO	Nguyen Tu Lap (NGUYENX TUR LAAPR)	Cpt
XO	Nguyen Van Tinh (NGUYEENX VEAN TINHL)	Sr. Cpt
PO	Nguyen Van That (NGUYEENX VEAV THAATS)	Cpt
APO	Nguyen Xuan Nguyen (NGUYEENX XUAAN NGUYEN)	Sr. Cpt

Combat Staff Asst   Loi (LOIL)
QM Staff Asst   U (UW)
Manager   Ngo (NGO)
Radio Operator   Xich (XICHS)

C-3, K-3

CO   Huynh (HUYNHL)
XO   Loan (LOAN)
PO   Minh (MINH)
APO   Huyen (HUYEENL)
Manager   Bang (BEANGL)

C-2, K-3

CO Do Van Thuoc (DOOX VEAN THUOWC)   1 Lt
XO Nguyen Van Bang (NGUYEENX VEAN BANG)   2 Lt
PO Nguyen Hoang Dan (NGUYEENX HOANG DANS)   1 Lt
APO Nguyen Van Xuyen (NGUYEENX VEAN XUYEEN)   Cpt
Manager
    Nguyen Van Tho (NGUYEENX VEAN THOOS)   Sgt
Doctor
    Bui Huy Chay (BUIL HUY CHAAYR)   Sgt
Rado Oper
    To (TOOS)
    Cham (CHAMS)
    Ly (LY)
    Thinh (THINHY)

B-1, C-2

Plt Ldr   Khuat Van Ngoc (KHUAATS VEAN NGOCV) (SOURCE)
A-1 Sqd Ldr   Vinh (VINH)
A-1 Asst Sqd Ldr Khue (KHUEE)
A-1 Sqd members Thi (THI),
                 Doan (DOANL),
                 Van (VEAN),
                 Ngu (NGUWX),
                 Xam (XAAM)

A-2 Sqd Ldr		Thuan (THUAAN)
A-2 Asst sqd ldr	Mi (MI)
A-2 Sqd members	Ao (AO),
			Nghia (NGHIAR),
			Tanh (TANHS),
			Thang (THEANGS),
			Trung (TRUNG)

			B-2, C-2
Plt Ldr		Ton Kiem (TOONL KIEEM)
Asst Ldr	Tan (TAAN)
Sdr Ldr		Dinh (DINHV)
Sqd Ldr		Kharh (KHANHS)

x. MORALE: Ngoc said that the men of C-2 were not bitterly discouraged. They feel the ARVN'S and the Americans will never really do them harm and are positive that the allies will not be able to find their firing points. The food supply is fairly constant although they have had a few hard times.

y. MISCELLANEOUS: (Knowledge of other enemy forces) - Ngoc stated that as of DOC, there was some unknown element of SR-5 located at YT020665. He located one cache of the 81st RSG at XT9868.

Source led American units to the former C-2 and C-3 base areas. On these missions, the Americans located and seized a firing tube of an 82mm mortar (vic. YT139628) as well as one DK-75 (vic. YT076608).

In May 1970, Ngoc attended a meeting of F-64 Regimental Command held at Katum. All the leaders of F-64 and the 75th Division listed in this report were present

z. SPECIFIC EEI:

1. What does the individual know about Suoi Nhung? In 1969, C-2 was located in an area which necessitated crossing the Suoi Nhung to go on a supply run to Man Tung. In 1969, Ngoc saw many NVA in

the vicinity of Suoi Nhung, but he could not identify these units. The C-2 doctor, Chay told Ngoc that K-13, a hospital, is located a 3-4 day walk from C-2 base area (as of Aug 1970). K-13 is located near Suoi Nhung (exact location unknown).

2. When travelling East on resupply missions, did he travel along stream beds and if so, what direction did the stream run (E-W, N-S)? What were the trail directions? Ngoc stated that it was a 4 - 5 day walk from C-2 to Man Tung. There is a trail running between these points. This trail is intersected by numerous trails and streams and has so many intersections that it would be impossible to recall any one specifically.

3. What contact did he have with the 47th Transportation Group? Ngoc denied knowledge of the 47th Trans Gp.

4. How far can he travel on a resupply mission in one day? Source stated that the entire trip from C-2 to Man Tung took 4 - 5 days. From POC (YT062612) to C-2 (XT983664) was approximately a one day walk.

5. What unit provides personnel to guide him into the 1st Bde AO? C-2 provided its own guide.

6. What does the normal 81st RSG food cache complex look like? What is the usual layout? Ngoc stated that he was familiar with only one 81st RSG cache (previously discussed in this report). Since he had never been allowed access to the cache itself, Ngoc could not diagram the internal structure of the site.

7. Where was the nearest hospital supporting his unit? Where do they take the wounded and where are the graves? The nearest hospital is K-13A (see no #1 EEI). As a general practice, C-2 buries its KIA's in a place not adjacent to C-2 area. There are no grave sites near the most recent C-2 area, for the unit has suffered no recent losses.

8. When will your unit stand and fight and when will it decide to evade? What are the circumstances? (see TACTICS v #4).

9. Does he have any knowledge of civilian or political proselytizing activities against U.S. troops? Ngoc stated that he was aware of such activities conducted by NVA as well as VC, but he was not entirely knowledgeable in this area.

10. (a.) What knowledge does he have on Directive 750? None.
    (b.) What knowledge does he have of Campaign 'X'? None.
    (c.) What knowledge does he have of Dry Season Operations? As of DOC, C-2 received no orders pertaining to Dry Season Operations.

11. Does he have any knowledge of K-17 Military District (VC)? No.

12. Does he have any knowledge of B-11/S-21? Ngoc had never heard of B-11, but he stated that approx. 10 month prior to DOC, the 81st RSG had changed its name to S-21. However, Ngoc feels that not all NVA/VC units are aware of the change, for some elements of the 81st RSG still refer to themselves as the 81st. Ngoc said that he believed that the S-21 HQ is located in Bing Long (location unknown) as of DOC.

13. Does he have any knowledge of Sapper Companies of SR-5? Ngoc stated that C-2 has no direct contact with SR-5. He said he had no information regarding Sapper Companies.

   a. INTERROGATORS EVALUATION:

   (1) DATE AND PLACE OF INTERROGATION: Source was interrogated numerous times between 20 Oct - 1 Nov 1970, at Camp Gorvad, RVN.

   (2) PHYSICAL AND MENTAL CONDITION OF SOURCE: Physically he appears in good health, mentally, he is quick-witted and intelligent.

   (3) ASSESSMENT OF SOURCE: As Ngoc began to co-operate with the interrogators, he was afforded many comforts. It seems he is now convinced that it is in his best interest to be truthful. He is quite

intelligent and knowledgeable and seems to be a militarily oriented man.

(4) INTERROGATOR/INTERPRETER: Johnson/Han
Lovelock/Nam/Tho
2nd ARVN MID Team

21 October 1970

1. Operations Summary:

The POW that E Troop captured on 20 October proved to possess a wealth of information concerning the mortar and recoilless rifle attacks conducted against Camp Gorvad. One of the NVA soldiers E Troop killed was Chief of Survey for the K-33 Artillery Battalion. Documents captured included a map annotated with the firing positions around Camp Gorvad, firing tables and a drawing of Camp Gorvad proper.

The POW volunteered to go on the ground and lead the Blues to the place where the 75mm recoilless rifle was buried. E Troop picked up the POW and conducted an over-flight of the area where he was captured. He was not sure of his directions and could not relate ground features from the air. E Troop discontinued the over-flight and conducted saturation reconnaissance of the area within 10000 meters of where the POW was captured. This reconnaissance resulted in the detection of a well-used trail and the Troop Commander decided to insert the Blues with the POW, on the trail, and walk in the direction of where the POW was captured.

The Blues were inserted at 1208 hours at YT092604. Following the trail, the Blues moved in a westerly direction until the POW suddenly recognized where he was on the ground. Once the POW was oriented, he moved with a determined purpose, informing the Blue Platoon Leader that the weapon was a 1000 meter stretch down the trail. At 1605 hours the POW told the Platoon Leader to stop, pointed to a spot on the ground and told the Platoon Leader that 75mm was buried there. The platoon dug one foot into the ground and found the recoilless rifle. The find consisted of the rifle and the ground mount for the weapon, with no sight. The POW stated that there was no sight for it and that the ammunition was stored elsewhere. The Blues moved to a PZ at YT073612 and were extracted at 1625 hours.

C Troop at YT176422 observed and engaged one (1) VC attempting to evade the Pink Team, resulting in 1 VC KBH. Later in the day, at YT735902 they observed and engaged another VC attempting to evade, resulting in 1 VC KBH.

A Troop at 0800 hours, in the vicinity of YU580074, observed 1 NVA walking along a trail. They engaged resulting in 1 NVA KBH.

At 0810 hours the Squadron received a request from the 3rd Brigade for a Combat Tracker Team. This team was to support F Troop, 2-11 ACR, which was OPCON to the 3rd Brigade. This unit had established contact with an unknown size enemy force. They found a blood trail and called for the Combat Trackers. The team was inserted and started to follow the tracks. The enemy had evaded through two streams in an effort to lose the trackers. Upon crossing the second stream, the dog alerted; indicating the presence of an enemy force. The team was engaged and the point and cover men returned fire. The team got results of 1 NVA KIA and 1 automatic weapon position destroyed. The enemy inflicted four (4) WIA on the Tracker Team. After contact had been re-established, the team was extracted at 1320 hours. A follow-up to this action resulted in the dog 'Otis' receiving the Bronze Star with 'v' device.

2. Task Organization:

No change

3. Intelligence Summary.

No change

4. Activities Statistics:

a.	Airmobile Operations	Insertions	Extractions
	Ranger Teams	3	2
	CTT Teams	2	2
	Blues	2	2

b. Aircraft Firings   HIT   NOT HIT   CRASHED/DESTROYED
    Negative aircraft firings today

c. Friendly Losses   Enemy Losses

KIA	0	KBH	4
WIA	4	KIA	1
MIA	0	WIA	0
		VCS	0
		NVAC	0
		KBAFA	2
		KBARTY	0
		KBAS	0

22 October 1970

1. Operations Summary:

E Troop was still exploiting the information given by the POW captured on 20 October. After the 75mm recoilless rifle had been captured, the POW (who by now had picked up the name of the 'Dude') offered to lead the Blues to the location of a buried 82mm mortar. On the night of the 21st he was interrogated and indicated a spot on the map where he felt the mortar was buried. He was picked up at 0800 hours by the Troop Commander and flown over the area. Again he was confused and could not relate anything on the ground to what he observed from the air. Again the scouts were sent out to locate any signs of recent activities in the area he had selected on the map. The scouts reported a trail in the vicinity of YT151625. The Blues along with the 'Dude' were inserted at 1215 hours at YT151625. By 1500 hours the 'Dude' indicated he didn't recognize anything on the ground and was lost. The Blues continued South along the trail and finally came to a wrecked, yellow logging truck. The 'Dude' now knew where he was and indicated they had been moving in the wrong direction. They should have been moving North instead of South. As it was getting late in the afternoon, the Blues prepared a PZ by chopping down trees. The Blues were extracted at 1630 hours from YT141637.

The Troop Commander took the 'Dude' and the Blue Platoon Leader on another visual reconnaissance, but to no avail. The 'Dude' just didn't recognize anything on the ground from the air. He drew a map of the general area where the mortar was buried and that's all he could do in attempting to locate the spot. He was returned to Camp Gorvad for the night. His sketch map is shown below.

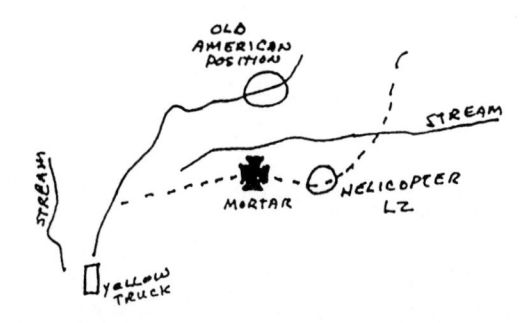

2. Task Organization:

No Change

3. Intelligence Summary:

No change

4. Activities Statistics:

a. Airmobile Operations Insertions Extractions
    Ranger Teams   3   3
    CTT Teams   1   1
    Blues   1   1

b. Aircraft Firings HIT   NOT HIT   CRASHED/DESTROYED
    Negative aircraft firings today

c. Friendly Losses   Enemy Losses
    KIA   0   KBH   0
    WIA   0   KIA   0
    MIA   0   WIA   0
                                VCS   0
                                NVAC   0
                                KBAFA 0
                                KBARTY 0
                                KBAS   0

23 October 1970

1. Operations Summary:

E Troop concentrated on locating the site of the buried mortar. At 1400 hours the White Platoon Leader had located the area that the 'Dude' had sketched the night before. At 1500 hours the Blues were en route to be inserted but adverse weather cancelled the insertion.

2. Task Organization:

No change

3. Intelligence Summary:

No change

4. Activities Statistics:

a. Airmobile Operations   Insertions   Extractions
   Ranger Teams   1   3
   CTT Teams   1   1
   Blues   0   0

b. Aircraft Firings   HIT   NOT HIT   CRASHED/DESTROYED
   Negative aircraft firings today

c. Friendly Losses   Enemy Losses
   KIA   0   KBH   0
   WIA   0   KIA   0
   MIA   0   WIA   0
                              VCS   0
                              NVAC   0
                              KBAFA   0
                              KBARTY   0
                              KBAS   0

*Author's Note: You were always taking a risk when you put the Blues on the ground. The normal size of a Blue Platoon was from 15 to 30 men. As a Troop Commander you had to consider METT. How urgent was the Mission, what was the Enemy situation, what type of Terrain were you putting them into, and what additional Troops did you have available to bail them out if they got into trouble. In this case they were out of the range of supporting artillery and due to the weather it was unlikely we could reinforce them with additional troops if they got in trouble.

24 October 1970

1. Operations Summary:

At 1211 hours E Troop inserted the Blues and the 'Dude' into a single ship hover down LZ at YT143617. As soon as they were on the ground the 'Dude' recognized the area and immediately started leading the Blues along a trail into a thick bamboo thicket. Once in the thicket the Blues came upon a deserted bunker complex. The 'Dude' moved to an area and told the Blues to start digging. Within a couple of minutes the Blues had uncovered the 82mm mortar tube. Within a couple of feet of this spot they located the tripod but were unable to locate the base plate. The Blues were extracted at 1435 hours.

With the capture of the mortar, all indirect fire attacks against Camp Gorvad ceased. Camp Gorvad did not receive incoming again until 21 December 1970. A total of 71 days passed without Camp Gorvad receiving an indirect fire attack. This was the longest period of time the camp had gone without receiving incoming since 1966!

A Troop and B Troop both received a mission of ground reconnaissance and inserted their Blues.

2. Task Organization:

No change

3. Intelligence Summary.

No change

4. Activities Statistics.

a. Airmobile Operations	Insertions	Extractions
Ranger Teams	2	2
CTT Teams	0	0
Blues	3	3

b. Aircraft Firings HIT NOT HIT CRASHED/DESTROYED
   A Troop   1
   C Troop   1

c. Friendly Losses   Enemy Losses
   KIA   0   KBH   0
   WIA   0   KIA   0
   MIA   0   WIA   0
                      VCS   0

25 October 1970

1. Operations Summary

At 1030 hours D Troop was called on the radio by a Pink Team from E Troop. E Troop requested that the 'Resource Control Point' personnel (who were mounted in gun jeeps) be sent to YT038648 to check out a large number of personnel who were located in an unauthorized area. D Troop responded and detained 52 personnel These personnel were turned over to GVN officials for classification at Phouc Vinh.

A Pink Team from A Troop, while following a trail, at 1200 hours, observed and engaged 2 VC hiding in the jungle next to the trail. This resulted in 2 VC KBH. The team continued to follow the trail as it showed recent use. As the scout hovered over the trees, his observer detected 2 more VC hiding in the jungle next to the trail. He immediately engaged them with his M-60 machine gun, resulting in 2 more VC KBH.

At 1430 hours Ranger Team #52 reported hearing movement of an enemy force moving toward their position. They remained in their concealed position waiting for the enemy force to bypass them. The force moved directly into their position and the team engaged them. In the fierce exchange of fire that followed, the team drove off the enemy force, who left behind, one (1) of their dead. The team had only one body left at the site but undoubtedly had inflicted more casualties. There were no casualties on the Ranger Team and they were later extracted.

2. Task Organization:

No change

3. Intelligence Summary.

No change

4. Activities Statistics

a. Airmobile Operations   Insertions   Extractions
   Ranger Teams   3   4
   CTT Teams   0   0
   Blues   0   0

b. Aircraft Firings HIT   NOT HIT   CRASHED/DESTROYED
   Negative air craft firings today.

c. Friendly Losses   Enemy Losses
   KIA   0   KBH   5
   WIA   0   KIA   1
   MIA   0   WIA   0

This map shows the stationing of Air Cavalry assets from 26 October through 30 November 1970.

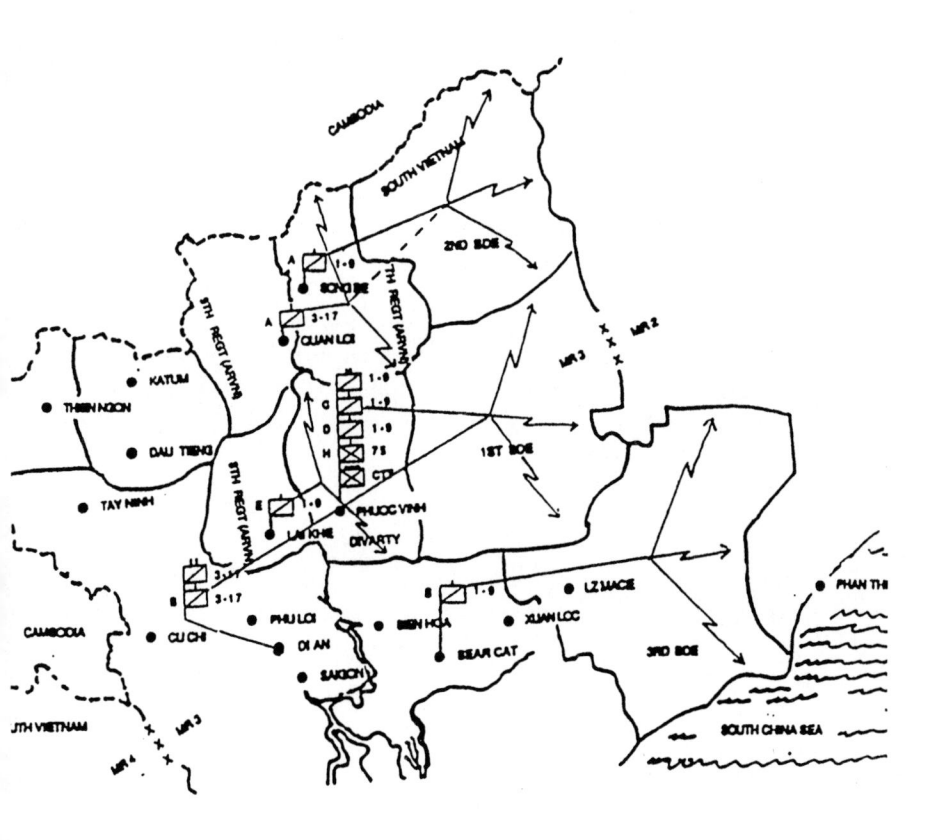

26 October 1970

1. Operations Summary

On this date the 3-17 Air Cavalry Squadron (ACS) (-) was placed OPCON to the 1st Cavalry Division. C Troop of the Squadron was attached to the 1-5 Mechanized Division at Quang Tri, and D Troop of the Squadron was attached to the 11th ACR.

The Headquarters and B Troop are stationed at Di An, with A Troop stationed at Quan Loi.

At the time the 3-17th was placed OPCON to the various units, The 1st Cavalry Division was tasked to provide Air Cavalry support to the 7th ARVN Regiment of the 5th ARVN Division.
Areas of responsibility were assigned to B/3-17 and A/3-17, based on their geographic location in the AO. A/3-17 was tasked to support the 7th ARVN Regiment and on order reinforce A/1-9 in supporting the 2nd Bde. of the 1st Cavalry Division. B/3-17 was tasked to support the 1st Bde., 1st Cavalry Division, along with C/1-9.
Responsibilities for each Squadron were spelled out in FRAGO 0297-Z (Tab G). Special tasks assigned each squadron are listed below.

(1) 1-9 ACS

a. Continue as co-ordinating Headquarters for Air Cavalry employment in the AO.

b. Release Operational Control of B and C Troops to 3-17 ACS.

C. Assume OPCON of A/3-17.

d. Support 2nd Bde., DIVARTY, and 7th ARVN Regt. on a priority task.

(2) 3-17 ACS

a. Release OPCON of A/3-17 to 1-9 ACS.

b. Assume OPCON of B/1-9 and C/1-9.

c. Support 1st and 3rd Brigades on a priority basis.

d. Station A/3-17 at Quan Loi.

Upon being placed OPCON to the Division (1st Cavalry Division), it was decided that it would be in the interest of both Squadrons, if cross training was conducted between the Squadrons to better understand how each Squadron worked. To accomplish this, E/1-9 and A/1-9 exchanged teams with A/3-17 for a period of 3 days at a time. B/1-9 and C/1-9 exchanged teams with B/3-17 for 3 day periods also. It was found that generally the Squadron's Operating Procedures were similar except for the employment of the Blue Platoons. This was due to the fact that units they (3-17 ACS) had worked with in the past had been unwilling to provide the QRF and the RRF to reinforce the Blues. It was also found the 3-17 Blues were not rappel qualified. This required that A/1-9 and C/1-9 train A/3-17 and B/3-17 respectively, on how to rappel the Blues from Lift aircraft. This training was accomplished within a week.

At 1400 hours the Squadron Commander, Troop Commanders and the S-3 of TF 1-9 had a meeting with the 7th ARVN Regimental Commander and his staff. At this meeting Air Cavalry tactics and techniques were discussed with emphasis being placed on the employment of the Blue Platoons. The ARVN Commander agreed to provide a QRF and a RRF whenever the Blues were on the ground, conducting ground reconnaissance.

At 1300 hours A/1-9 observed and engaged one (1) NVA at YU220412. This resulted in one (1) NVA KBH.

At 1500 hours C/1-9 observed two (2) individuals on a logging truck in an unauthorized area. The Blues were inserted, picked up these individuals and after extraction they were detained at Phouc Vinh.

2. Task Organization:

BDE CONTROL	TF 1-9 Control	TF 3-17 Control
D/1-9	HQ 1-9	HQ 3-17
H Co. 75th Rangers	A/1-9	B/3-17
62nd CTT	E/1-9	B/1-9
	A/3-17	C/1-9

3. Intelligence Summary:

No change

4. Activities Statistics:

a.
Airmobile Operations	Insertions	Extractions
Ranger Teams	4	0
CTT Teams	2	2
Blues	1	1

b.
Aircraft Firings	HIT	NOT HIT	CRASHED/DESTROYED
B Troop		1	

c.
Friendly Losses		Enemy Losses	
KIA	0	KBH	1
WIA	0	KIA	0
MIA	0	WIA	0
		VCS	2
		NVAC	0
		KBAFA	0
		KBARTY	0
		KBAS	0

1 - 11 November 1970

1. Operations Summary.

During the first 11 days of November there was no change in Task Organization or concept of operations. Both Squadrons conducted reconnaissance in assigned areas with scattered contact throughout the AO. By keeping constant pressure throughout the AO the Squadrons were successful in denying the enemy unmolested access through the area. Utilizing the Blue Platoons to conduct recon missions on intelligence the Pink Teams had gathered, and the Rangers to provide surveillance in designated areas, the pressure on the enemy was kept at a high level.

2. Task Organization:

No change

3. Intelligence Summary:

No change

4. Activities Statistics:

a. Airmobile Operations

	Insertions	Extractions
Ranger Teams	20	18
CTT Teams	10	10
Blues	37	37

b. Aircraft Firings

	HIT	NOT HIT	CRASHED/DESTROYED
A Troop		2	
B Troop	2		1
E Troop	3		1
A/3-17		5	
B/3-17		2	

c. Friendly Losses   Enemy Losses
   KIA   0   KBH   26
   WIA   7   KIA   0
   MIA   0   WIA   1
                            VCS   0
                            NVAC   0
                            KBAFA   0
                            KBARTY   0
                            KBAS   0

12 November 1970

1 - Operations Summary.

On this date, the 1-9 picked up responsibility to provide Air Cav support to the 9th ARVN Regiment of the 5th ARVN Division. Although the Regiment was responsible for this area, most of the Regiment was involved in operations in Cambodia. This meant the A/3-17 now had to co-ordinate with the local and regional forces located in the 9th Regt's AO. This proved to be a difficult task. The Troop attempted to co-ordinate clearances to fire and found that none of the advisors would give clearance to fire. If the Troop talked to District they were told to talk to Province. If the Troop talked to Province they were told to talk to District. It finally required the 5th ARVN Division Headquarters to get involved, and they directed that District Headquarters give the required clearances. Once this was cleared up, A/3-17 assigned an LNO at the District Headquarters for the remainder of the time they were there.

2. Task Organization:

No change

3. Intelligence Summary:

The 9th ARVN AO contains part of the Serges Jungle Highway, a major supply route from Cambodia to SR-5 and is trafficked by members of the 83rd Rear Services Group. Their suspected location and cache sites are felt to be in the area of the Michelin Plantation.

4. Activities Statistics:

a. Airmobile Operations Insertions   Extractions
   Ranger Teams   2   0
   CTT Teams   0   0
   Blues   0   0

b. Aircraft Firings HIT   NOT HIT   CRASHED/DESTROYED
   C Troop   1

c. Friendly Losses   Enemy Losses
   KIA   0   KBH   1
   WIA   0   KIA   0
   MIA   0   WIA   0
                           VCS   0
                           NVAC   0
                           KBAFA 0

13-30 November 1970

1. Operations Summary

During this period both Squadrons had scattered contact throughout the Division's (5th ARVN) (1st Cavalry) AO. A/3-17 supported the 7th and 9th Regiments (ARVN) and on three days (during this period) supported the 2nd Brigade operations along the border. During these same three days A/1-9 was supporting operations in the Dragonheads area of the 2nd Brigades AO. B/3-17 reinforced B/1-9 in the 3rd Brigade AO in addition to working the Eastern part of the 1st Brigade AO.

These changes in areas of interest were directed by the issuance of verbal FRAGO'S. Usually the areas of interest were decided after the evening Division (1st Cavalry Division) briefing. When acting in a reinforcing role, the Troop that was reinforcing would be directed to provide a designated number of Pink Teams to the Troop they were reinforcing. The Troop that was reinforced assumed OPCON of those teams at first light. They released OPCON of them at last light.

On 15 November, A/3-17 terminated support to the 9th ARVN Regiment.

Author's Note: On 27 November, E Troop (provisional) 3-17 Air Cavalry Squadron was formed from the assets of the 334 Attack Helicopter Company and was stationed at Di An. They were formed similar to the formation of E/1-9 in that they received equipment and personnel from the other troops of the 3-17 Air Cavalry.

2. Task Organization:

BDE. CONTROL	TF 1-9 Control	TF 3-17 Control
D/1-9	HQ 1-9	HQ 3-17
H Co. 75th Rangers	A/1-9	B/3-17
62nd CTT	E/1-9	B/1-9
	A/3-17	E/3-17

3. Intelligence Summary. Aerial surveillance by VR aircraft continues to deny the enemy freedom of his resupply routes. It is felt that a severe food shortage is being felt by the enemy units in the 2nd Bde. AO as evidenced by the recent increase in ralliers from the K-14 area.

4. Activities Statistics:

a.
Airmobile Operations	Insertions	Extractions
Ranger Teams	25	25
CTT Teams	21	21
Blues	76	76

b.
Aircraft Firings	HIT	NOT HIT	CRASHED/DESTROYED
A/1-9	2	6	1
B/1-9	1	2	
C/1-9	1	1	
E/1-9	1	3	
A/3-17	0	5	
B/3-17	1	3	
E/3-17	0	2	

c.
Friendly Losses		Enemy Losses	
KIA	0	KBH	40
WIA	14	KIA	9
MIA	0	WIA	0
		VCS	9
		VCC	0
		NVAC	0
		KBAFA	2
		KBARTY	0
		KBAS	2

A comparison of the statistics for the 1st Cav Div is reflected below. This comparison reflects the percentage of kills for the 9th Cavalry Brigade in contrast to the rest of the Division.

	AUG	SEP	OCT	NOV
Div. Total	197	232	221	169
9 Bde Total	80	126	121	76
9 Bde Initiated Kills	114	150	143	91
9 Bde % of Division Totals	34	54	54.8	44.9
9 Bde % of Initiated Kills	64.3	64.6	64.7	53.8

This map shows the stationing of Air Cavalry assets from 1 December through 24 December 1970.

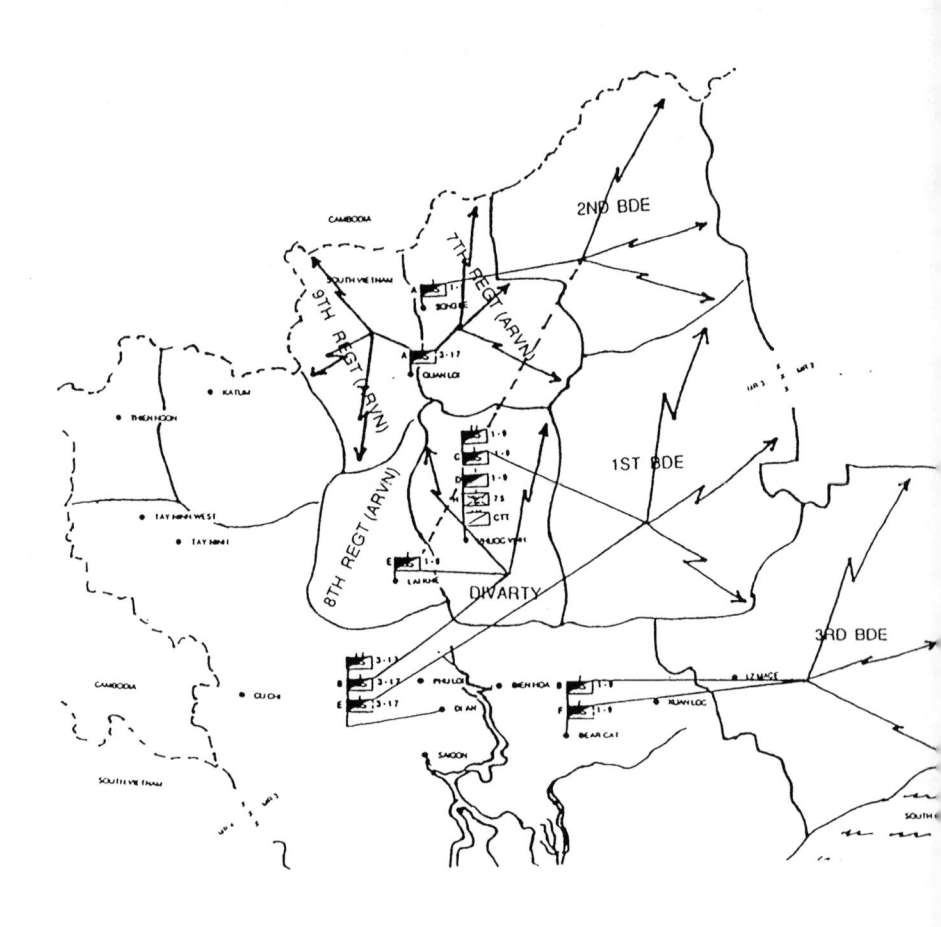

1 - 6 December 1970

1. Operations Summary.

From the first of the month to the sixth there was scattered contact throughout the Division AO. Air Cavalry continued to seek out and destroy the enemy throughout the AO.

Author's Note: On 5 December a Division FRAGO was received (Tab J) which officially formed the 9th Air Cavalry Brigade (Provisional) and formed F Troop 1-9, both effective 8 December 1970.

2. Task Organization:

No change

3. Intelligence Summary.

No change

4. Activities Statistics:

a. Airmobile Operations   Insertions   Extractions
    Ranger Teams   10   9
    CCT Teams   7   7
    Blues   27   27

b. Aircraft Firings   HIT   NOT HIT   CRASHED/DESTROYED
    Negative aircraft firings

c. Friendly Losses   Enemy Losses
   KIA   2   KBH   2
   WIA   6   KIA   2
   MIA   0   WIA   0
                           VCS   23
                           NVAC   0
                           CSWC   1
                           IWC   1
                           KBAS   4

7 December 1970

1. Operations Summary.

On this date A Troop completed a road sweep from Song Be to Don Xoai to Duc Phoung, while the rest of the Brigade continued visual reconnaissance of the Division AO. Twice B Troop took fire on aircraft. Insertions were at a high level but no contact was established.

2. Task Organization:

No change

3. Intelligence Summary:

No change

4. Activities Statistics:

a. Airmobile Operations	Insertions	Extractions
Ranger Teams	0	1
CTT Teams	1	1
Blues	6	6

b. Aircraft Firings	HIT	NOT HIT	CRASHED/DESTROYED
A Troop		1
B Troop		2
E Troop		1

c. Friendly Losses
KIA 0
WIA 0
MIA 0

Enemy Losses
KBH 5
KIA 0
WIA 0
VCS 1
NVAC 0
KBAFA 0
KBARTY 0
KBAS 0

8 December 1970

1. Operations Summary.

During the day, boundary changes were passed to all troops. The major conflict of the day was with Ranger Team #52, at YS807935. They spotted 2 Viet Cong, moved closer to them and then spotted one structure with 4 other individuals. They then engaged the 2 VC and received small arms fire in return. The engagement left 1 VC KIA and negative friendly casualties. The other VC evaded to the South.

* Author's Note: On this date the 9th Air Cavalry Brigade (Provisional) became official and F Troop 1-9 was formed from D/229th Assault Helicopter Battalion and was stationed at Bear Cat.

2. Task Organization:

BDE. CONTROL	TF 1-9 Control	TF 3-17 Control
D/1-9	HQ 1-9	HQ 3-17
H Co. 75th Rangers	A/1-9	B/3-17
62nd CTT	A/3-17	B/1-9
	E/1-9	C/1-9
	E/3-17	F/1 - 9

3. Intelligence Summary.

No change

1. Activities Statistics:

a. Airmobile Operations Insertions Extractions
   Ranger Teams   2   2
   CTT Teams   1   1
   Blues   1   1

b. Aircraft Firings HIT NOT HIT CRASHED/DESTROYED
   A/1-9   3

c. Friendly Losses   Enemy Losses
- KIA   0   KBH   0
- WIA   0   KIA   1
- MIA   0   WIA   0
-                VCS   0
-                NVAC   0
-                KBAFA 0

9 - 22 December 1970

1. Operations Summary

During this 13 day period the Brigade kept the enemy alert by many small contacts and Blue's insertions. A boundary change affecting 3rd Bde. was sent to B/1-9 and E/1-9 on 11 December. There seemed to be a rash of mechanical problems to the Squadron aircraft of the 1-9th.

The enemy was kept moving throughout the AO and was constantly sought out resulting in many aircraft being fired upon. C/1-9 reported finding 600lbs. of rice and 200lbs. of rice was picked up by E Troop. The largest find (rice cache) of that period was by E Troop who located 1500lbs. of rice on 19 Dec 1970.

During this period four new fire support bases were opened in the DIVARTY AO.

2. Task Organization:

No change

3. Intelligence Summary

The 2300lbs. of rice found and destroyed by the troops during the period placed a greater strain on the enemy's supply system.

Activities Statistics:

a. Airmobile Operations	Insertions	Extractions
Ranger Teams	17	13
CCT Teams	1	1
Blues	71	71

b. Aircraft Firings

	HIT	NOT HIT	CRASHED/DESTROYED
B/1-9	2	4	1
C/1-9			1
E/1-9	1		1
F/1-9		1	
A/3-17		1	
B/3-17		1	
E/3-17		4	

* Author's Note: On 15 December, E Troop was using their maintenance Huey to sling load out an LOH that had been shot up that day. As the maintenance aircraft cleared the pad at about 200 feet, the lift hook opened and the LOH fell to the ground completely destroying the LOH. There was no explanation as to what had caused the malfunction other than perhaps static electricity.

c. Friendly Losses   Enemy Losses
   KIA   1   KBH   11
   WIA   12   KIA   4
   MIA   0   WIA   0
                       VCS   2
                       VCC   1
                       KBAFA   0
                       KBARTY   0
                       KBAS   0

23 - 24 December 1970

1. Operations Summary.

On 23 Dec 1970 the Brigade published OPLAN 2-71 which was a plan designed to provide security for the Bob Hope show (The OPLAN follows this day's activities).

On 24 December the Brigade received a be prepared mission to send up to two air cavalry troops to support the 2nd ARVN Airborne Brigade, due to the build up of enemy forces along the border north of Thien Ngon. The Troop(s) sent on this mission would most likely move to Tay Ninh.

2. Task Organization:

No change

3. Intelligence Summary.

No change

4. Activities Statistics:

a. Airmobile Operations	Insertions	Extractions
Ranger Teams	1	5
CTT Teams	1	1
Blues	4	4

b. Aircraft Firings	HIT	NOT HIT	CRASHED/DESTROYED
C/1-9			1
A/3-17		2	1

c. Friendly Losses   Enemy Losses
   KIA   0   KBH   0
   WIA   0   KIA   0
   MIA   0   WIA   0
                           VCS   0
                           NVAC   0
                           KBAFA   0
                           KBARTY   0
                           KBAS   0

CLASSIFICATION

No Change From Verbal Orders

                        Copy 15 of 16 copies 9th
                        Air Cavalry Brigade
                        Phouc Vinh XT962491
                        RVN 230800 December 1970

OPLAN 2-71

Reference Map Series L607 Vietnam Sheet 6330, 6331, 6430, 6431.

Time Zone used throughout the order: HOTEL

Task Organization:

TF 1-9	TF 3-17	BDE. Control
A/1-9	B/3-17	H Co. 75th (Rngr)
A/3-17	B/1-9	62nd Inf. Plt. (CTT)
E/1-9	C/1-9	D/1-9
E/3-17	F/1-9	

1. Situation. The Bob Hope show will tour Vietnam again this year, and will present a performance for the First Cavalry Division at Curry Amphitheatre (YT062057). The unclassified name for this is, Operation Holly. Commencing on D-1 elements of the First Cav will preposition to move to the Amphitheatre and the units from Phouc Vinh will return to Phouc Vinh after the show. Elements of the 3rd Bde. will remain overnight at Bien Hoa and return to LZ Mace on D+1.

    a. Enemy Situation:

    (1) The enemy possesses the capability of conducting mortar and rocket attacks against Curry Amphitheatre.

(2) See current INTSUM for D day.

b. Friendly Situation:

(1) The First Cavalry Division will conduct air and ground convoys to move 2150 troops to Curry Amphitheatre on D Day. The Division will augment the security forces protecting the Amphitheatre by providing two (2) Air Cavalry Troops in support of the Bien Hoa sector (ARVN) and the RTAVF.

(2) III Corps (ARVN) will conduct extensive patrols in Bien Hoa province within 25 KM of Curry Amphitheater to preclude the enmy use of rockets or mortars against curry Amphitheater during the performance.

c. Attachments and Detachments:

(1) Attachments: None
(2) Detachments: Red Plt., Blue Plt. D/1-9.
    (a) Red Platoon OPCON DIVARTY 0600 hrs. D Day.
    (b) Blue Platoon remains OPCON 3rd Bde.

2. Mission. 9th Air cavalry Brigade will continue present mission, provide convoy escort for convoys to and from Phuov Vinh and LZ Mace, and place one Air cavalry Troop in support of ben Hoa sector (ARVN) and one Air Cavalry Troop in support of the RTAVF. Be prepared tp reinforce two Air cavalry Troops in support of ARVN and RTAVF forces, and act as a QRF to both convoys.

3. Execution.

a. Concept of operation. On D-1 (D Day to be announced 72 hours in advance of performance) place one Air Cavalry Troop in support of RTAVF. On D Day provide one cavalry platoon as convoy escort and from Camp Gorvad and one Cavalry Platoon as convoy escort from LZ Mace. The Brigade (-) will provide a QRF for each convoy. On D+1 one Cavalry Platoon will provide convoy escort from Bien Hoa Army base to LZ Mace.

b. TF 1-9

(1) Continue present mission.

(2) Place E/3-17 in support of Bien Hoa sector, effective 0700 hrs. D-1 until 2000 hrs D Day.

(3) Provide QRF, on order, to convoy that originates at Phuoc Vinh.

c. TF 3-17

(1) Continue present mission.

(2) Place B/1-9 in support of RTVAF, effective 0700 hrs. D-1 until 2000 hrs D. Day.

(2) Provide QRF, on order, to convoy that originates at LZ Mace.

d. D/1-9 (-)

(1) Place Red Platoon OPCON to DIVARTY, effective 0600, D Day until release back at Phouc Vinh.

(2) Blue Platoon continues in support of 3rd Bde.

e. Co-ordinating instructions.

(1) OPLAN 2-71 becomes OPORD 2-71, effective 0700 hrs. D-1.

(2) Troop Commanders supporting ARVN and RTAVF forces will co-ordinate directly with supported units NLT 230800 Dec. 70.

(3) LNO's will be provided the supported ARVN and RTAVF units. The supporting Air Cavalry Troops will provide the LNO'S.

(4) Direct co-ordination is authorized between TF's and convoy commanders.

4. Service Support: OPORD 1-71.

5. Command and Signal

a. Index T-13 SOI.
b. Brigade CP will remain at Phuoc Vinh XT962491.

Acknowledge.

                                                        NEVINS
                                                        LTC

OFFICIAL:

CHOLE
S-3

Distribution: A

This map shows the stationing of Air Cavalry assets on 25 December 1970.

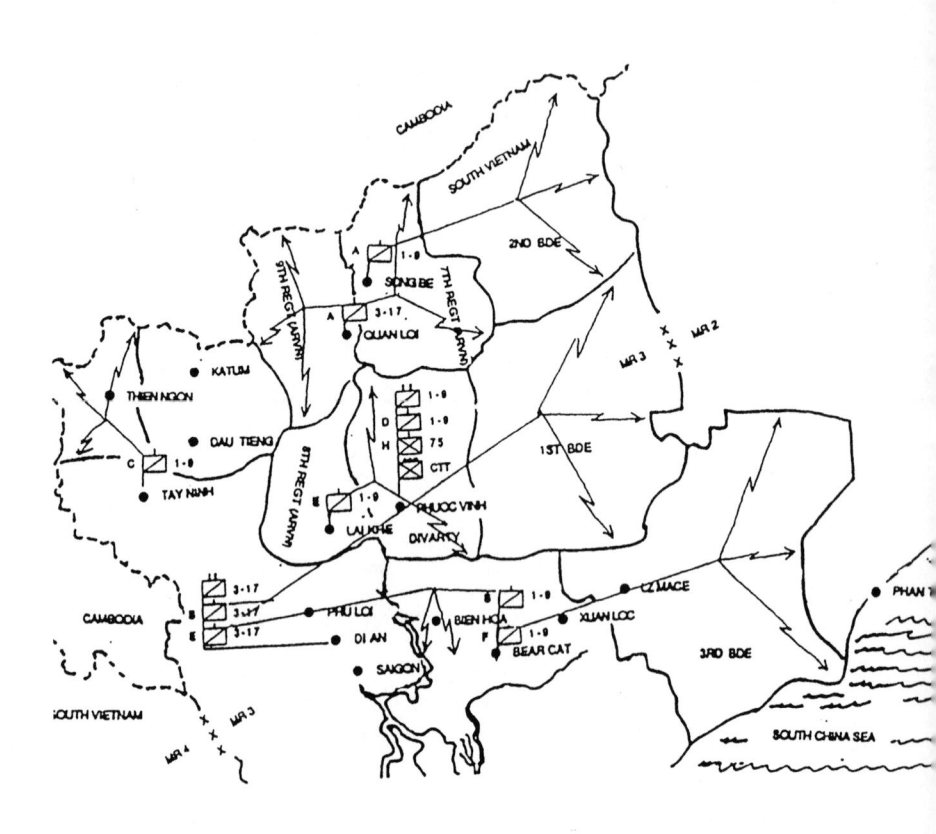

25 December 1970

1. Operations Summary:

The morning of the 25th found Operation Holly in full swing. B/1-9 and E/3-17 were involved in providing security for the Bien Hoa area in support of the Bob Hope show. On the night of the 24th the Brigade was alerted to a possible commitment of two Air Cavalry Troops to the Tay Ninh area. C/1-9 and E/1-9 were alerted to a possible change of mission. Each Troop Commander was called to Brigade Headquarters and received a briefing on possible areas of employment. They also received maps of the area around Tay Ninh. At 0830 hours TF 1-9 Commander and the Brigade S-3 were en route to Tay Ninh when a call was received from Division Headquarters informing the Brigade to send one Air Cavalry Troop to Tay Ninh. TF 1-9 Commander called the C/1-9 Commander and informed him to move the combat elements of his troop to Tay Ninh as soon as possible. At 1045 hours the combat elements of C Troop arrived at Tay Ninh and by 1400 hours that day had established contact with the enemy. For planning purposes C Troop was to remain at Tay Ninh for three days. The Troop remained at Tay Ninh from 25 December through the end of this reporting period, 15 February 1971.

2. Task Organization:

No change

3. Intelligence Summary:

No change

4. Activities Statistics:

a. Airmobile Operations	Insertions	Extractions
Ranger Teams	0	0
CTT Teams	0	0
Blues	1	1

b. Aircraft Firings HIT   NOT HIT   CRASHED/DESTROYED
   Negative aircraft firings

c. Friendly Losses   Enemy Losses
   KIA   0   KBH   3
   WIA   1   KIA   1
   MIA   0   WIA   0
                           VCS   0
                           VCC   0

This map shows the stationing of Air Cavalary assets from
26 December through 30 December 1970.

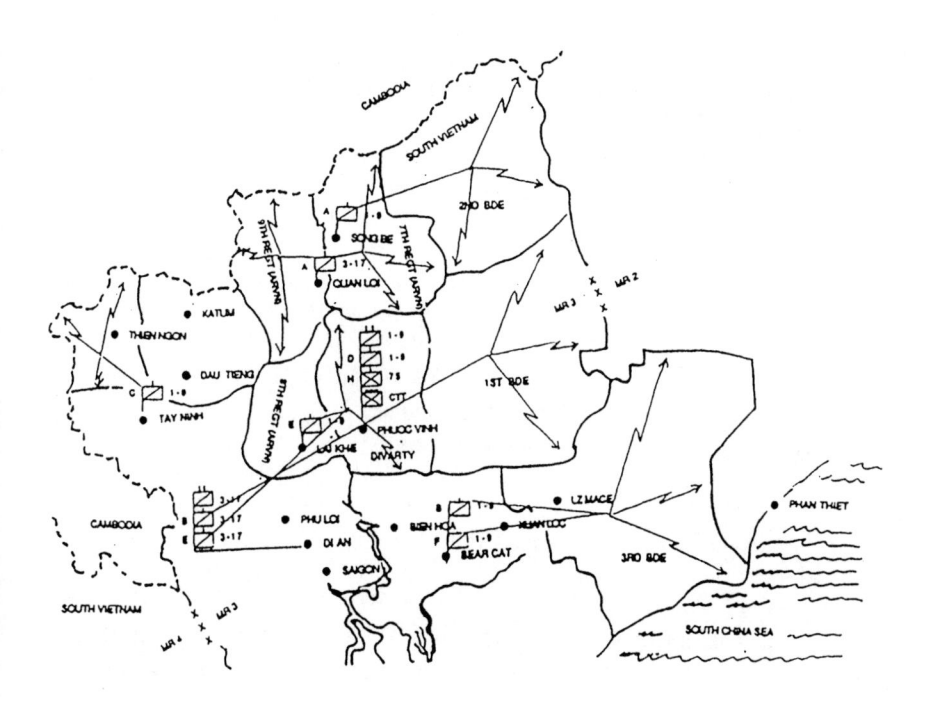

26-30 December 1970

1. Operations Summary

Daily contact with the enemy characterized this period of operations. On 28 December A/1-9 inserted the Blues in the 9th ARVN Regiment area of operations to conduct ground reconnaissance in an area where a Pink Team had reported recent movement. After insertion the Blues were engaged by an estimated company size element. Due to problems encountered in getting permission to insert the ARVN QRF the decision was made to pull out the Blues and engage the enemy force with fire power. Prior to extraction the Blues confirmed two enemy KIA and two enemy Killed By Helicopter. After the Blues were extracted the area was engaged with AFA, artillery and air strikes. Results of this engagement were never confirmed as there was no follow-up by ARVN forces. Also during this period Ranger Team #22 established contact with an unknown size enemy force which resulted in unknown enemy personnel losses and the capture of 3 rucksacks, 125 pounds of rice, 2 gallons of U.S. cooking oil, 3 ponchos and a note book.

In the 8th ARVN Regiment's area of operation E/1-9 encountered helicopter booby traps placed in trees. One booby trap detonated but did not damage the aircraft.

It was during this period that an OH-58 from B/3-17, while flying low level, struck a high tension line, crashed and burned, killing all crew members on board.

On 29 December the Brigade received a be prepared order to conduct a Cavalry Raid in an attempt to rescue Allied Prisoners of War.

2. Task Organization.

No change

3. Intelligence Summary:

The enemy continues to use defensive tactics only, and avoids contact when possible.

4. Activities Statistics:

a. Airmobile Operations　Insertions　Extractions
　　Ranger Teams　　　　12　　　　　8
　　CCT Teams　　　　　　2　　　　　2
　　Blues　　　　　　　　9　　　　　9

b. Aircraft Firings　HIT　NOT HIT　CRASHED/DESTROYED
　　A/1-9　　　　　　1　　3
　　B/1-9　　　　　　1　　2
　　E/1-9　　　　　　1　　　　　　　　1

c. Friendly Losses　　　Enemy Losses
　　KIA　3　　　　　　KBH　　8
　　WIA　1　　　　　　KIA　　2
　　MIA　0　　　　　　WIA　　0
　　　　　　　　　　　　VCS　　2
　　　　　　　　　　　　VCC　　0
　　　　　　　　　　　　NVAC　0
　　　　　　　　　　　　KBAFA 0
　　　　　　　　　　　　KBARTY 0
　　　　　　　　　　　　KBAS　1

This map shows the stationing of Air Cavalry assets on 31 December 1970

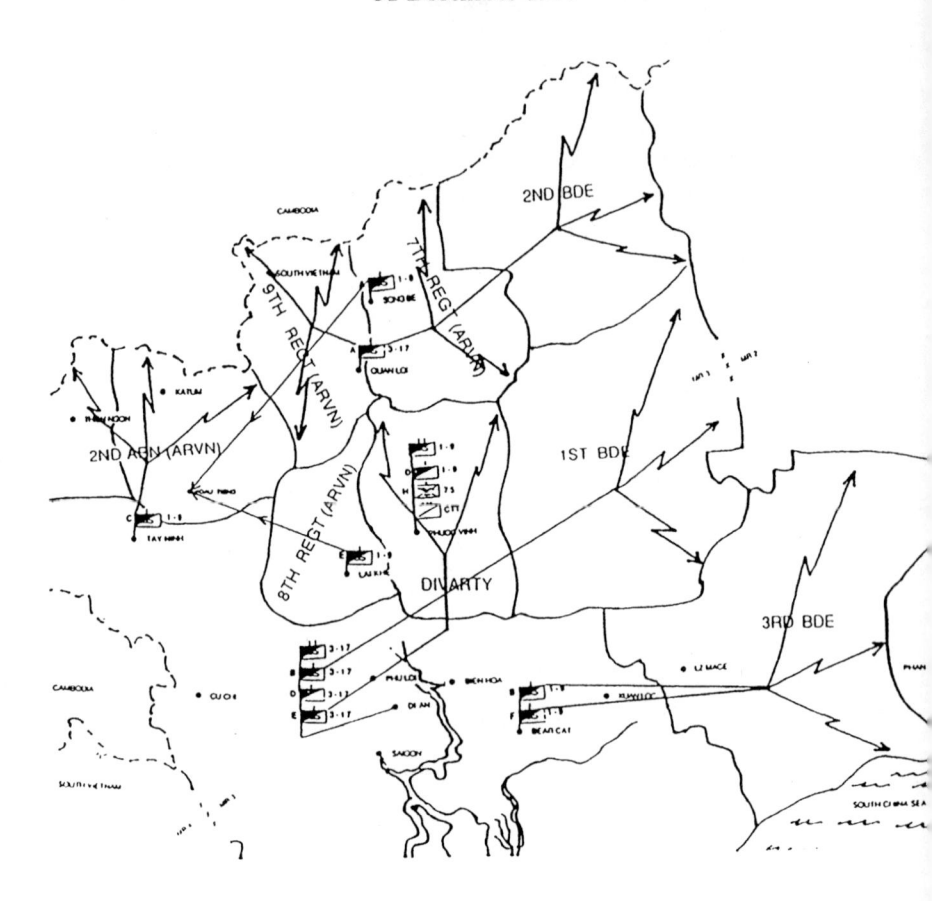

31 December 1970

1. Operations Summary:

This day was highlighted by the operations of TF Nevins. This Task Force was organized to locate and rescue allied prisoners of war reportedly located near Dau Tieng, Vietnam. This operation was a classic Air Cavalry Raid. The Operations Order and After Action Report follows this day's activities.

D/3-17 returned to the 3-17 Squadron and was assigned to TF 3-17.

2. Task Organization:

BDE. Control	TF 1-9	TF 3-17	TF NEVINS
D/1-9	HQ/1-9	HQ/3-17	A/1-9
H Co. 75th (Rgr)	C/1-9	B/3-17	E/1-9
62nd (CTT) (-)	A/3-17	B/1-9	2-12 Inf (-) (OPCON)
	E/3-17	F/1-9	C/2-20 AFA (OPCON)
		D/3-17	One LZ Const. Tm (OPCON)
			2 Medevac AC (OPCON)
			One CTT
			TAC Air (Strip alert)
			TAC Air (LZ Const.)
			Psyop (Strip alert).

3. Intelligence Summary.

The end of the year found the 9th Brigade flying in the following provinces:

Binh Tuy (3rd Bde)
Long Khanh (1st Bde)
Upper Phouc Long (2nd Bde)
Upper Binh Duong (DIVARTY)
Western Phouc Long (7th ARVN Regt)
Binh Long (9th ARVN Regt)

Tay Ninh (2nd ARVN Abn Bde)

Contact with the enemy remains at low level and the extensive visual reconnaissance by the 9th Brigade has effectively denied the enemy access to cross border supply points. Ralliers within the Tactical Area of Operations indicate that the enemy is stressing food production and the use of woodcutters to supply badly needed food. Hoi Chanhs (Enemy soldiers who give up using a safe conduct pass) and POW's also indicate the lack of food or resupply. In Binh Tuy Province, the 33rd NVA Regt. has established a Shadow Supply System (SSS) which provides food and medicine through the use of civilian travellers with GVN identification. Eagle Flights working in conjunction with National Police Check Points are reducing this means of resupply.

* Author's Note: Eagle Flights (also referred to as Hawk Flights) consist of one Huey with a rifle squad, accompanied by one scout aircraft and one weapons aircraft who cruise a selected area looking for suspicious people. The scout would operate low level (as he always did) and check everyone in the AO. If the scout determined there was a suspicious person that needed to be picked up and talked to, he would call the Huey (who, until needed, was flying at altitude with the gun ship) who swooped down, landed, the Blues picked up the person, and put him or her on the Huey. At the end of the mission (normally two hours of flight time) they flew to the nearest POW collection point or Police check point and turned over all the personnel they had picked up for interrogation.

It is felt however, the 33rd NVA Regiment is still the best provisioned of all enemy units within the AO and continue to avoid contact with allied elements.

4. Activities Statistics

a. Airmobile Operations	Insertions	Extractions
Ranger Teams	1	1
CTT Teams	3	3
Blues	3	3

b. Aircraft Firings HIT   NOT HIT   CRASHED/DESTROYED
   Negative aircraft firings

c. Friendly Losses   Enemy Losses
   None   None

A comparison of the statistics for the 1st Cav Div is reflected below. This comparison reflects the percentage of kills for the 9th Cavalry Brigade in contrast to the rest of the Division.

	AUG	SEP	OCT	NOV	DEC
Div. Total	197	232	221	169	140
1-9 Total	80	126	121	76	49
1-9 Initiated Kills	114	150	143	91	63
1-9% of Division Totals	34	54	54.8	44.9	35
1-9 % of Initiated Kills	64.3	64.6	64.7	53.8	45

DEPARTMENT OF THE ARMY
HEADQUARTERS, 1ST SQUADRON (AIRMOBILE) 9TH CAVALRY
1ST CAVALRY DIVISION (AIRMOBILE)
APO San Francisco 96490

AVDARS - 3   1 January 1971

SUBJECT: After Action Report TF NEVINS

See Distribution

1. Background: On 29 December 1970 this Headquarters received a be prepared mission to conduct an operation designed to locate and free a group of prisoners located in the Razor Back area North of Dau Tieng RVN. A usually reliable source has indicated that 20 to 30 allied prisoners of war were located in the vicinity of XT509576 (Primary location, point 20 on attached map). Secondary locations for the POW camp were at XT442579 (point 21 on map) or at XT483532 (Point 22 on the map).

2. The Brigade task organized as shown.

BDE CONT	TF 1-9	TF 3-17	TF NEVINS
D/1-9	HQ/1-9	HQ/3-17	A/1-9
H Co. 75th (Rgr)	C/1-9	B/3-17	E/1-9
62nd (CTT) (-)	A/3-17	B/1-9	2-12 Inf (-) (OPCON)
	E/3-17	F/1-9	C/2-20 AFA (one sect.)
		D/3-17	(OPCON)
			One LZ Const. Tm. (OPCON)
			2 Medevac Aircraft (OPCON)
			One Combat Tracker Team
			TAC Air (Strip alert Bien Hoa)
			TAC Air (LZ Const.)
			Psyop (Strip alert Bien Hoa)

LZ Two Bits, November 1967, RVN
The Author receives his first Distinguished Flying Cross from Major General John J. Tolson, CG 1st Cavalry Division (Airmobile)

Photo: U.S. Army

*Jump Command Post for Task Force Nevins
31st December 1970, Dau Tieng, RVN*

Waiting to be called
31st December 1970, Dau Tieng, RVN
Combat Tracker Team

Waiting for word the prisoners have been located
31st December 1970, Dau Tieng, RVN
Left to right: LT CMDR McFaden (USN) (JPRC) (MACV); MAJ
Chole, Brigade S3; LTC Nevins, 9th Brigade and TF Commander;
CPT Fountain, Brigade S4

Major General George W. Putnam Jr.
Commanding General 1st Cavalry Division (Airmobile)
at the time of this report.

Photo: U.S. Army

Brigadier General Johnathon R. Burton
*Assistant Division Commander 1st Cavalry Division (Airmobile) at the
time of this report*

Photo: U.S. Army

Commanders 1-9 Cavalry
Left to Right: CPT Al Ferria, A Troop; CPT John Ritter, E Troop; MAJ Claude Lott, B Troop; LTC Robert Nevins, Squadron Commander; MAJ Doug Erway, outgoing commander B Troop; MAJ Keith Ball, C Troop; CPT Frank Stewart, H Co 75th Rangers; CPT Ron Beyer, Headquarters and Headquarters Troop.

Photo: U.S. Army

COMMANDERS AND STAFF OFFICERS 9TH CAVALRY BRIGADE

Back Row Left to Right: LT Byer (3-17); CPT Richmond (3-17); CPT Cook (1-9); CPT Schlain (3-17); CPT Ricks (1-9); LT Jones (1-9); CPT Lockast (3-17); Chaplain Pass (1-9); Command Sergeant Major Stump (1-9)

Front Row Left to Right: CPT Hendrick (3-17); MAJ Mack (3-17); MAJ Rafferty (3-17); LTC Williams (CO 3-17); LTC Nevins (CO 9th BDE); LTC Putnam (CO 1-9); MAJ Chole (1-9), CPT Fountain (1-9)

Photo: U.S. Army

3. Discussion:

   a. Sequence of events:

   The operation commenced at 0645 hours when A/1-9 and E/1-9 converged on the areas of interest the morning of the 31st. Pink Teams of each Troop saturated the areas of interest at points 20, 21, and 22. E/1-9 was responsible for the eastern portion of the AO and the primary target area. A/1-9 was responsible for the western portion of the AO and one secondary area of interest. The visual reconnaissance produced no evidence of a POW compound in the primary or secondary areas of interest.

   The Troops expanded their area of search and at 0925 hours A/1-9 located a bunker complex at point one (on the map), and observed three to five individuals in black clothing. Observing the rules of engagement (Annex B), the team did not engage but continued observation while awaiting the arrival of the Blues. The team selected an LZ and at 0930 hours received ground to air fire from point 2 (on the map). At 0944 the Blues were inserted near the ground to air firing point and moved to the south-east towards the bunker complex. They arrived in the bunker complex at 1215 hours and reported finding fifteen camp fire sites with some of the fires still burning. There were numerous cooking utensils in the area and the Blues estimated 20 to 30 individuals had used that area this morning. Although there had been recent activity in the area there was no indication that this was a POW compound. The three to five individuals that had been in the area successfully evaded.

   While this activity was taking place the remainder of the Air Cavalry Troops continued their search for the POW compound. A/1-9 had detected another bunker complex south of the river opposite point 2 (on the map). Based on the trail activity in the area and the number of bunkers located on the south side, an AO extension was requested to the 40 North South grid line. This extension was approved. At 1030 hours A/1-9 received ground to air fire from point 3 (on the map) in the vicinity of the bunker complex, and at 1215 hours they received ground to air fire from point 4 (on the map). At 1240 hours B/2-12 was inserted at point five (5) and moved to the Southeast toward the bunker complex located near point 3 (on the map).

When B/2-12 was inserted a directive was dispatched to Phouc Vinh to extract one platoon of C/2-12 and bring them forward to Dau Tieng, and be prepared to act as the QRF. The remainder of C/2-12 was in PZ posture ready for extraction and movement forward as the situation dictated.

At 1440 hours E/1-9 Blues were inserted at point 6 (on the map) and conducted ground reconnaissance to the west in an effort to detect the presence of the POW compound.

At 1425 hours while moving to the Southeast B/2-12 located a three foot wide trail running east to west showing signs of recent use by an undetermined number of individuals. The Company paralleled the trail and located a latrine with human waste approximately five (5) minutes old. The Second Platoon was point element for the Company and went on line at this time and swept approximately ten (10) metres when they were engaged by small arms fire and one (1) light machine gun. The Company attempted to flank the enemy position from the west but were stopped by heavy bamboo, RPG, and AK-47 fire. Throughout the engagement the Company was engaged by B-40, small arms, and hand grenades.

Concurrent with this action A/1-9 Blues were moved back to a PZ in the vicinity of point 2 (on the map) and were extracted at 1507 hours and reinserted at 1525 hours at point 7 (on the map) to act as a blocking force. The weapons aircraft from A/1-9 were supporting the contact and a section of AFA was bounced from Dau Tieng to assist in the contact area.

B/2-12 remained in contact throughout this period until 1730 hours when contact was broken. At 1646 hours the decision was made to break contact, pull back and hit the area with Tactical Air. Due to the dense undergrowth and heavy volume of fire, it took the Company approximately forty five minutes to break contact entirely.

While this was in progress E/1-9 extracted their Blues at 1710 hours and returned them to Dau Tieng. The ground reconnaissance by

E/1-9 Blues confirmed the fact that there was no POW compound located in the primary area of interest.

To assist in the contact area two more sections of AFA from 2-20 were called forward from Phuoc Vinh; this gave the TF a total of three AFA sections.

At 1735 hours a scout aircraft from A/1-9 went to the contact area to mark for an airstrike that was on station. While marking the target area he observed one NVA soldier standing in the doorway of a bunker. He engaged, resulting in one NVA KBH. His weapons aircraft fired into the area and a check of the area revealed another KBH. At 1745 the airstrike was placed upon the position resulting in five NVA KBAS, three 3' X 5' bunkers with overhead cover destroyed. The Scout while performing BDA of the airstrike observed one dazed and wounded NVA. He engaged resulting in one more NVA KBH. While performing the BDA two more NVA were killed by AFA outside of the airstrike area.

Following the airstrike B/2-12 moved back to a PZ and was extracted at 1830 hours. A/1-9 Blues were extracted from point 7 at 1815 hours. Results of this contact were: three (3) NVA KBH, five (5) NVA KBAS, and two (2) NVA KBAFA, there were eleven (11) friendly WIA.

The cease fire for New Years went into effect at 1800 hours and upon completion of the Blues extraction A/2-12 returned to Song Be, B/2-12 and one platoon from C/2-12 were returned to Phuoc Vinh in CH-47 and UH-1 aircraft and E/1-9 remained at Dau Tieng with one Pink Team and the Blue Platoon until the area was cleared of all POL and ammunition. The operation was terminated at 1930 hours when the last element of the Task Force cleared Dau Tieng.

    b. Operations Planning.

    (1) The Operations Plan required that the QRF (one platoon) and the RRF (the remainder of the company) laager at Minh Thanh. This was changed twelve hours before the operation commenced to insure ease of control, and responsiveness. Locating the QRF and the RRF

with the forward TF CP facilitated briefing the RRF prior to insertion.

(2) In this particular operation the 'source' of information had no personal knowledge of the exact location of the POW camp. In future operations, of this type, it would be of assistance to the TF if the 'source' of the information were made available to go on the ground and lead the Blues to the POW camp.

(3) The Joint Personnel Recovery Center (JPRC) (MACV) has available a kit that includes bolt cutters and wire cutters. Lt. Cmdr. Mcfadyen from JPRC brought this kit to the TF CP and instructed the Blues on the operation of the equipment.

4. Conclusion:

    a. There were no POW compounds located at the primary or secondary areas of interest.

    b. This was an excellent mission for Air Cavalry, and is the type of mission Air Cavalry is well suited to perform.

5. Recommendation:

    a. In future raid missions of this nature, the operation should be conducted on a day that would allow for exploitation of any contact that develops. In this particular operation, the requirement to cease offensive operations at 1800 hours on 31 December 1970 severely limited the duration of our response to this contact.

    b. In future operations of this type, it is recommended that the 'source' of the information be compromized, paid a large sum of money as compensation, and be available at the forward CP and be used to lead the Blues to the POW camp.

    c. That the Operations Plan (Division) be amended to laager the QRF and RRF at the forward CP for ease of control and co-ordination.

    d. Lt. Cmdr Mcfadyen from the Joint Personnel Recovery Center (JPRC) (MACV) offered a great deal of assistance in the form of technical advice for the use of special equipment he made available to the operation. It is recommended that utilization of personnel from the JPRC, and this special equipment, be utilized on all such operations and this be written into the operation plan (Division).

/s/ Hilbert H. Chole
/t/ Hilbert H. Chole
Major, Armor
S-3

ANNEXES:

A - Map of the area of operations
B - OPLAN 1-70 (TF NEVINS)
C - Diagram of contact area for B/2-12

Distribution: A

Annex A to After Action Report - TF Nevins, 31 Dec 1970.

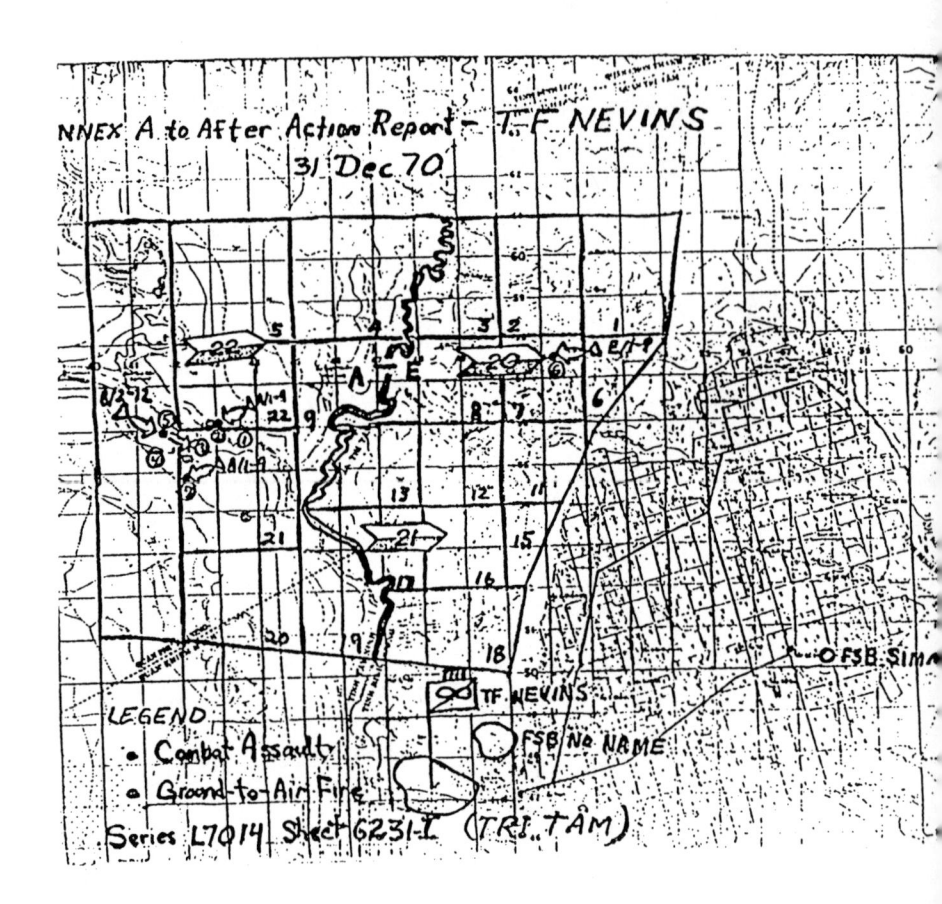

Annex B to After Action Report TF NEVINS

No change from verbal orders

Copy of Copies
TF NEVINS
Phuoc Vinh XT 962491
300800 Dec 1970
OF 004

OPLAN 1-70

References: Map series L607 Vietnam, Sheet 72311, 1:50000

Time zone used throughout the order: HOTEL

Task Organization:

TF NEVINS	RESERVE
E/1-9 Air Cav	2-12 Inf (-)
Two Pink Teams A/1-9 (OPCON)	C/1-9
B/2-12 Inf. (OPCON)	
One AFA Section (2-20 AFA) (DS)	
One Combat Tracker Team (DS)	
One LZ Construction Team (DS)	
One Medevac (with hoist, field extraction) (DS)	
One Medevac (back haul) (DS)	

1. SITUATION: A usually reliable source has indicated that 20 to 30 Allied Prisoners of War are located in the vicinity of XT509576 (primary location) or possibly at XT442579 or XT483532 (secondary locations).

   a. Enemy Situation:

   (1) Disposition: OB holding indicate that enemy units within the area of interest are directly responsive to SR-1.

   (2) Composition: Current intelligence estimates place the 35th

VC Arty Bn in the vicinity of XT498519 with an estimated strength of 140 (personnel). HQ and Support Rear Services Group 83 Vic. XT5755, estimated strength 291, 64th Dau Tieng Co. (VC), SR-1 vic. XT5048 estimated strength 50.

(3) Recent activity in the area of interest. On 24 December 1970 a platoon of 1-8th ARVN on a ground reconnaissance established contact with an estimated squad size element at XT543474. This contact resulted in two VC KIA. The unit was identified C-1 9th Sapper Bn., 429th Sapper Command.

(4) Analysis and discussion:

(a) Analysis: Indicators are that the enemy has devoted his time to construction of multi-level bunkers in which to house the prisoners. Indicating a semi permanent POW camp.

(b) Discussion: A swift strike force with a pre-planned target would most likely meet with squad to platoon size resistance. The enemy course of action in the event they are attacked is as follows.

1. Release the prisoners, one guard per prisoner, and attempt to exfiltrate the contact area using the prisoners as hostage.

2. Kill the prisoners, blowing the bunkers on top of them and then break up into two man groups and attempt to evade the contact area.

3. Conclusions: All direct access routes to the POW camp will be monitored and/or booby trapped. There will most likely be dug in perimeter defensive positions, with initial determined resistance. However, a lack of recent activity in the area and a sense of security should find the enemy unprepared for a determined ground attack against the compound.

b. Friendly Situation:

(1) The 9th Air Cavalry Brigade continues its present mission and conducts operations to locate and free Allied Prisoners of War in assigned area.

(2) 25th ARVN Division continues present mission.

(3) 5th ARVN Division continues present mission.

(4) 11th CAG supports operations of TF NEVINS by providing necessary lift aircraft.

    c. Attachments and detachments: See Task Organization

2. MISSION: TF NEVINS conducts operations in assigned area of operation to locate and free Allied prisoners of war.

3. EXECUTION:

    a. Concept of operation.

(1) Maneuver: TF commences search to locate POW camp initially in assigned areas with visual reconnaissance teams. Teams will replace each other on station providing continuous coverage in assigned areas. When a positive target is located the Blues will be inserted to conduct ground reconnaissance, free the prisoners or act as a blocking force. If the Blues positively locate the POW compound the Infantry Company will be inserted to free the prisoners or act as a blocking force. If the Blues are in heavy contact the QRF will be inserted to reinforce the Blues. The remainder of the Company will be inserted, on order, to reinforce, free prisoners, or act as a blocking force.

(2) Fires. See Annex C

    b. E/1-9 Cav

(1) Launch maximum VR Teams available to cover assigned AO.

(2) Station time 0645 hours.

(3) Laager Blues at air strip at Dau Tieng Vic. XT492473.

(4) Provide continuous VR coverage in assigned area of

operation.

(5) Insert Blues to conduct ground reconnaissance, free the prisoners, or act as a blocking force.

c. B/2-12 Cav

(1) Conduct final extraction from present field location NLT 0700 hours D Day.

(2) Co-ordinate requirements for lift assets to conduct final extraction direct with 11th CAG.

(3) Move one platoon with 5 + 2 direct from field extraction point to the air strip located at Minh Thanh, aircraft will shut down, the platoon will remain on 5 minute strip alert and at the same time this Company will be OPCON to TF Nevins.

(4) The Company (-) will complete final extraction from present field location with an additional 5 + 2 to Chon Thanh Vic. XT768623. Turn around will be flown until extraction is complete.

(5) At Chon Thanh Co. (-) will be picked up by CH-47 and flown to Minh Thanh.

(6) Be prepared to reinforce Blues with the QRF on five minutes notice.

(7) Be prepared to Combat Assault to free prisoners of war or act as a blocking force.

d. 2-12 Cav (-) be prepared to reinforce ground operations with additional force and assume control of the operation on order from Division.

e. C/1-9 Cav be prepared to assume any part of E/1-9 Cav mission on order.

f. Co-ordinating Instructions:

(1) OPLAN 1-70 becomes OPORD 1-70, 0600 D Day.

(2) Blanket political and military clearance to fire will be obtained for area of operation effective 0600 D Day until termination of operations.

(3) Rules of Engagement: Due to the nature of this operation strict control of all fires must be observed. It is to be expected that the enemy as well as the prisoners of war will be dressed in similar attire, with that consideration in mind the following rules of engagement are established.

(a) There must be positive identification of all hostile elements, and an aggressive act must be initiated by the enemy before they are engaged.

(b) Aimed fire will be used in all cases except in response to an ambush.

(c) Recon by fire is prohibited.

(d) Every opportunity will be afforded the enemy to surrender.

(e) Aerial fires will be delivered against point targets in all cases except for LZ preps.

4. SERVICE SUPPORT. See Annex B

5. COMMAND AND SIGNAL

i. Current SOI, D Day in effect.
ii. Spot reports will be transmitted to TF CP frequency to be announced.
iii. TF CP located at Dau Tieng XT492473.
iv. Upon commitment of the second rifle company, 2-12 be prepared to assume control of the ground operation.

ACKNOWLEDGE:

NEVINS
LTC

OFFICIAL:

CHOLE
S-3

Annexes:

A - Operation Overlay
B - Service Support
C - Fire Support

Distribution: A

ANNEX A (Operations Overlay) to OPLAN 1-70

OVERLAY NOT AVAILABLE

ANNEX B (Combat Service Support) to OPLAN 1-70 TF NEVINS

Reference: OPLAN 1-70

Time zone used throughout the order: HOTEL

1. General. This order outlines the Combat Service Support for TF NEVINS located in the vicinity of ST492473.

2. Material and Service

a. Supply

(1) Class I.

(a) All elements will enter the objective area with two days rations.

(b) Class I resupply will be accomplished by TF NEVINS. Parent organizations will supply rations for their elements. 2-12 Inf. rations will be picked up at the Guess Who pad. 1-9 rations will be picked up at the Pine Ridge pad.

(2) Class II. A six (6) point POL point will be established at 310800 at Dau Tieng by the 11th CAG. Type POL available: JP - 4.

(3) Class V.

(a) All elements will enter the objective area with a basic load of ammunition.

(b) The ASP will be established at Dau Tieng NLT 310730. Resupply to the ASP will be as required.

(c) Types ammunition available:
1. 5.56mm 16,800
2. 7.62 16,000
3. 20mm (M-60) 8,000
4. 40mm 5,000
5. M-79 500
6. 45cal 300
7. 38cal 300
8. 2.75 Rockets 10lb. 300
9. 2.75 Rockets 17lb. 320
10. 2.75 Rockets Flechette 144
11. WP Grenades 48
12. Fragmentary Grenades 48
13. Concussion Grenades 48
14. Smoke Grenades 94

b. Transportation

(1) Upon execution of OPLAN 1-70 one platoon of B/2-12 (QRF) will be field extracted and moved to Minh Thanh Vic. XT6366732. 2-12 will co-ordinate this move directly with 11th CAG.

(2) B/2-12 (-) will be field extracted and moved to Chon Thanh Vic. XT768623. 2-12 will co-ordinate the move directly with the 11th CAG.

(3) Movement of B/2-12 (-) from Chon Thanh to Minh Thanh will be accomplished by the 11th CAG. Co-ordination for the move will be accomplished by TF NEVINS.

(4) TF NEVINS Jump CP will be operational at Dau Tieng 310645.

(5) LZ construction personnel will depart Pine Ridge Pad 310700 and will be on five minute alert at TF NEVINS Jump CP.

3. Medical Evacuation

   a. Field extractions will be made by 15th Med for ground casualties.

   b. Air crew members that become casualties will be medically evacuated to Phouc Vinh.

4. Personnel

   a. Allied POW's will be field extracted to Dau Tieng. TF NEVINS will transport Allied POW's to Phouc Vinh for processing.

   b. Enemy POW's will be field extracted to Dau Tieng. TF NEVINS will transport enemy POW's to Phouc Vinh for processing.

ANNEX C (Fire Support) to OPLAN 1-70
Reference: Map Series L607 Vietnam, sheet 6231 I, 1:50000

1. Situation

a. Enemy Forces: See current INTSUM

b. Friendly Forces.

TF NEVINS
E/1-9 (Reinforced)
A/2-12 Inf. (OPCON)

RESERVE
2-12 Inf. (- 1 Co.)
C/1-9 Air Cav

DIRECT SUPPORT
C/1-77 Arty (-) on call
B/2-20 AFA (1 Section)
One Combat Tracker Team
Engineer LZ Construction Team
Two Medevac

* Author's Note: The Task organization shown in this annex and the OPLAN itself, changed the day prior to the operation. Rather than reinforcing E Troop with two Pink Teams, A Troop assumed responsibility for half of the AO. Also the company 2-12 Inf provided was actually B Co.

2. EXECUTION

a. Concept of Operations.

(1) One section B/2-20 AFA to displace with the Task Force.

(2) One section B/2-20 AFA on strip alert at Camp Gorvad.

(3) 3 tubes C/1-77 Arty to displace on call and assume DS to

Task Force.

    b. Air Support: TAC air on strip alert Bien Hoa AFB.

    c. Artillery Support

        (1) ARVN

        (a) Dau Tieng (XT492473) 3 tubes 105mm

        (b) FSB Simmons (XT578503) 2 tubes 105mm

        (2) US: 3 tubes 105mm C/1-77 to provide FS on order. Location to TBA.

        (3) Aerial Field Artillery: B/2-20 AFA. One section Dau Tieng (XT492473), One section 2 minute alert at Camp Gorvad.

    d. Co-ordinating Instructions: All requests for fire to be passed to Crafty Tracker 52 (Arty LNO) on FM 42.85 for co-ordination. Request for fire to C/1-77 to be passed on FM 42.85, Spare Slapper 2 SL, for co-ordination when committed.

    3. ADMIN AND LOG

    a. ASP: Dau Tieng (XT492473) for AFA.

    b. Resupply: Dau Tieng (XT492473) Class III for AFA.

    4. COMMAND AND SIGNAL: Current SOI/SSI in effect.

Annex C (Sketch of Contact area B/2-12 Inf.)
to After Action Report TF NEVINS.

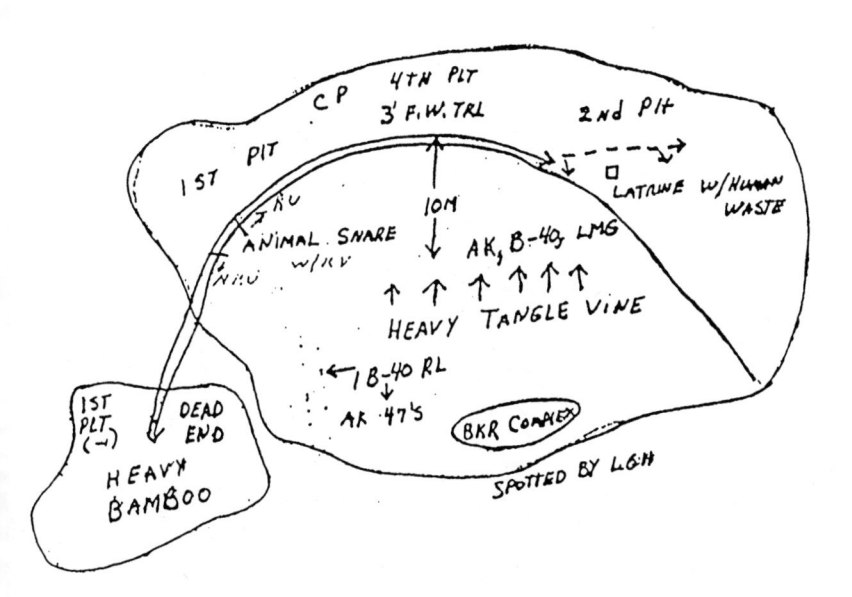

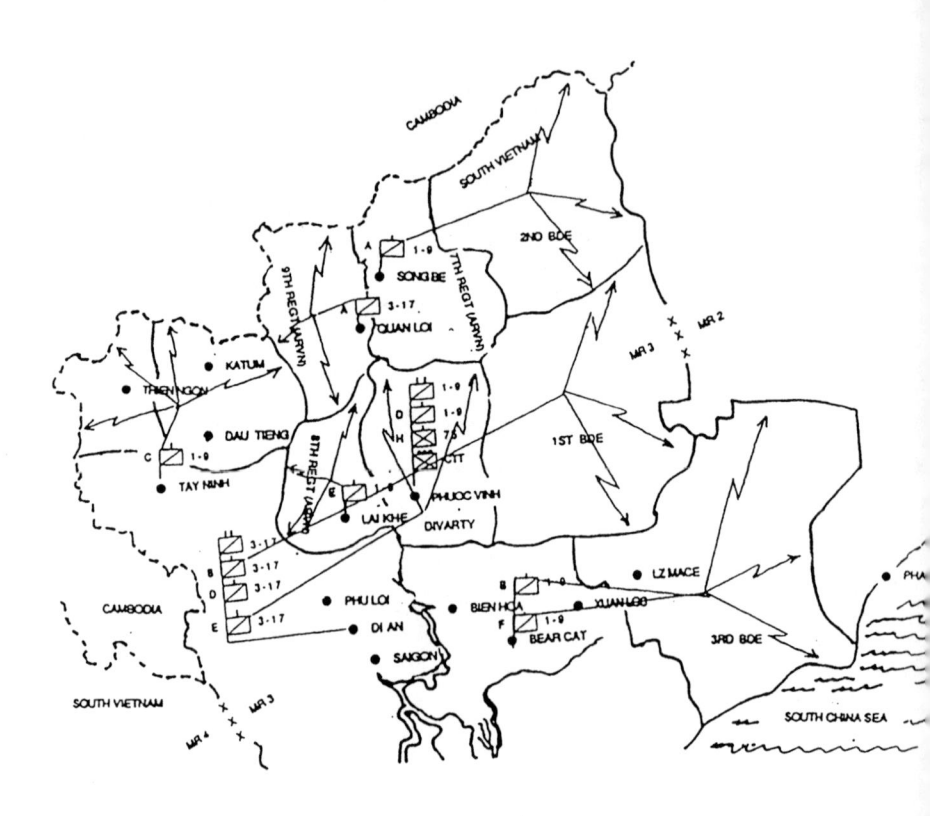

**This map shows the stationing of Air Cavalry assets on 1 January 1971.
(MAP 1)**

This map shows the stationing of Air Cavalry assets on 5 January 1971.
(MAP 2)

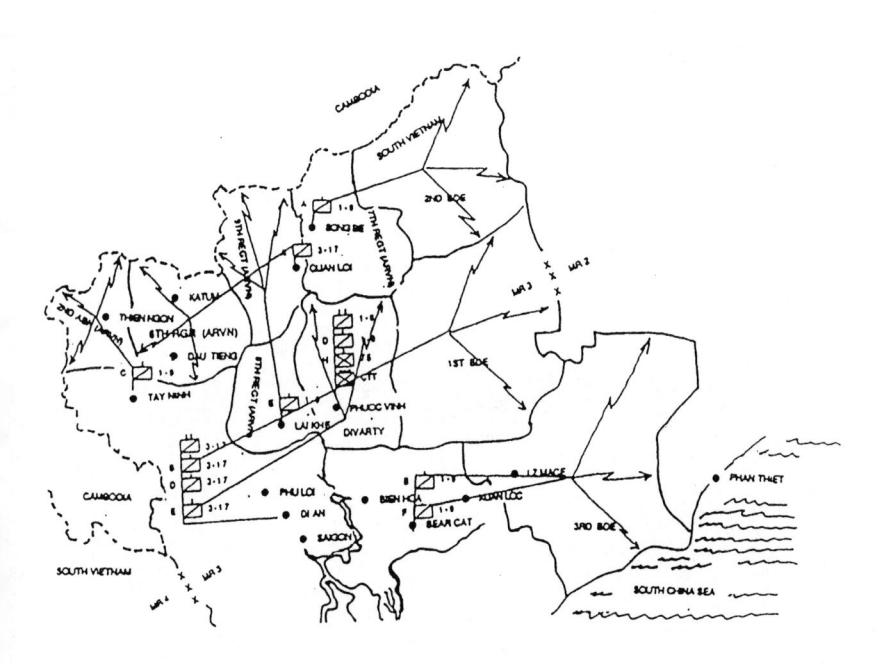

**This map shows the stationing of Air Savalry assets from
9 January through 31 January 1971.
(MAP 3)**

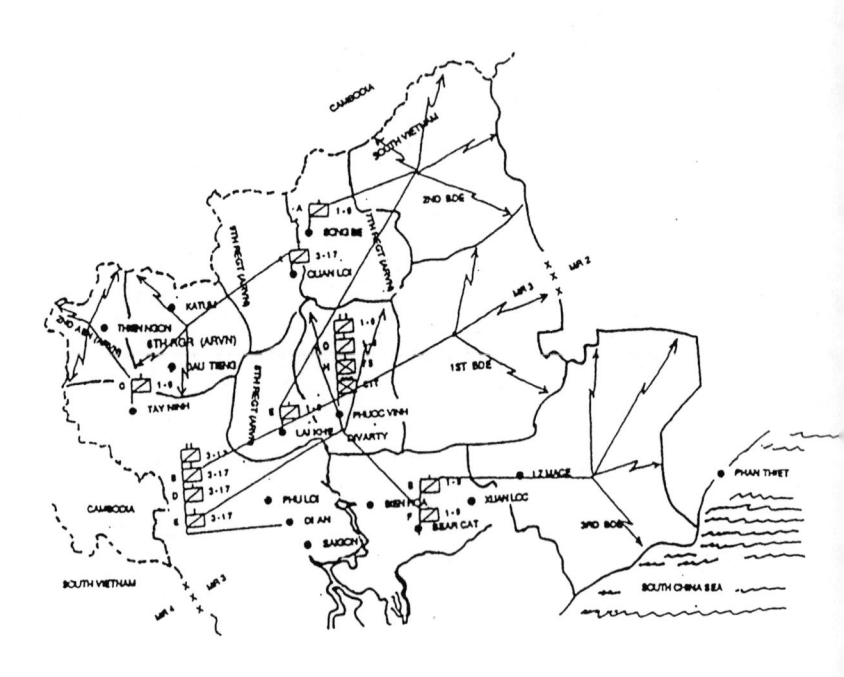

1 - 15 January 1971

1. Operations Summary:

This period of operations was characterized with frequent repositioning of Air Cavalry Troops. This repositioning posed no problems, as by this time, all Troops of the Brigade had the requirements for initial co-ordination and liaison down pat. The month began with the various troops supporting as shown on map 1. On 5 January 1971 the Brigade once again shifted troops as shown on map 2. The movement of the 6th ARVN Ranger Group into Eastern Tay Ninh Province resulted in II Field Forces Vietnam directing that they receive one Air Cav Troop to work with them. A/3-17 was designated to work with them. On 9 January the Brigade received a requirement to provide one Air Cavalry Troop to provide security for Admiral Moore's visit to Vietnam. At the same time, the Brigade was informed that E/3-17 was going to revert (back) to the 334 Attack Helicopter Company on 17 January. This resulted in the redeployment of F/1-9 into the DIVARTY AO and E/3-17 being tasked to provide security for Admiral Moore, followed by assignment to work in the 1st Brigade AO until deactivation. Map 3 illustrates the moves.

There was scattered contact throughout the period. Ranger Team 71 engaged 4 NVA moving through their area, resulting in 4 NVA KIA. Charlie Troop also received 122mm rockets in their Troop area at Tay Ninh. This attack by fire resulted in five troopers being wounded. E Troop discovered a concentration of NVA in their AO and in the process of engaging them lost a LOH to ground fire.

On 10 January 1971, in Eastern Tay Ninh Province, an ARVN convoy was ambushed by (suspected) 2 NVA Companies from the 271st VC/NVA Regiment. The VC/NVA companies were deployed on both sides of QL22. The report was received by C/1-9 and 3 Pink Teams responded within five minutes along with a section of AFA from 2-20 Arty. When the 3 Pink Teams from C Troop arrived on station they spotted 25 - 30 individuals evading to the West. They immediately engaged the target. When AFA arrived on station they also engaged. During this period one AFA aircraft received 2 hits from ground fire. The combined Cobra forces returned repeatedly to the area delivering accurate close fire support to the besieged convoy which had several vehicles destroyed and several KIA and WIA. After an Air Force air strike went into the area, the Pink Team performed a Bomb Damage Assessment (BDA). One LOH spotted a .51 calibre pit with weapon and immediately took fire from small-arms, sustaining several hits. The aircraft was forced to make a precautionary landing due to loss of all flight instruments. The Blues were inserted and secured the area.

Maintenance personnel were inserted for inspection of the aircraft, which was determined to be flyable. The aircraft was then flown out to Tay Ninh for repairs. Another Scout discovered 2 more .51 calibre pits. He directed the Cobras to engage the positions and they destroyed the positions. The action lasted 6 hours and terminated at darkness. A survey by ARVN ground forces produced 54 enemy killed. Of those, 35 were KBH (15 to C/1-9, 10 credited to 2-20 AFA).

The following day, another ARVN Convoy was ambushed from both sides of QL22. Again the enemy used .51 Calibre and RPG fire. 3 Pink Teams from C/1-9 again responded and within 5 minutes of being called were delivering fire on the enemy. This was followed almost immediately by two sections from the 2-20 AFA. The ARVN vehicles were repeatedly struck by RPG fire and the convoy was brought to a halt. The Cobras were making gun runs on both sides of the road and during these runs the Cobras came under .51 calibre fire from 2 positions. The Cobras repeatedly attacked these positions until the guns were silenced. This action lasted 5 hours. Darkness prevented further action by the air crews. Artillery was fired into the area during the night. This action resulted in another 15 NVA KBH.

2. Task Organization:

No change

3. Intelligence Summary:

Support of the 2nd ARVN Airborne Brigade in Tay Ninh Province has brought the 9th Brigade into contact with the 271st NVA

Regiment, newly arrived from Cambodia.

4. Activities Statistics:

a. Airmobile Operations   Insertions   Extractions
    Ranger Teams   28   26
    CTT Teams   11   11
    Blues   32   32

b. Aircraft Firings   HIT   NOT HIT   CRASHED/DESTROYED
    A/1-9   0   1
    C/1-9   11   10
    E/1-9   5   14   1
    B/3-17   0   3
    E/3-17   0   1

c. Friendly Losses   Enemy Losses
    KIA   0   KBH   69[4]
    WIA   7[5]   KIA   9
    MIA   0   WIA   4
                             VCS   2
                             VCC   0
                             NVAC   0
                             KBAFA   25
                             KBARTY   0
                             KBAS   4

---

[4] 7 of the enemy were found at a site of a contact by the ARVN.
[5] 5 WIA occurred when C Troop was shelled by 122 rockets.

16-19 January 1971

1. Operations Summary.

On 16 January 1971 Ranger Team 22 gained contact with an estimated VC Squad. As the Rangers approached a destroyed bunker they were engaged by approximately a squad size force. During the exchange of fire, one VC was KIA by the Team. They requested coverage by a Pink Team and they maneuvered to break contact. With the arrival of the Pink Team from B/3-17 they maneuvered against the enemy force. While screening their advance the LOH also received ground to air fire. Following this exchange, the Rangers were pulled back to a PZ and extracted. The area was engaged with artillery and AFA with no further assessment of the area.

On 17 January 1971, E/3-17 was disbanded and reverted to its original designation of the 334th Attack Helicopter Company.

On 18 January 1971, C/1-9, working with the 2nd ARVN Airborne Brigade at Tay Ninh Province, had a Pink Team locate 24 - 30 enemy moving East toward (highway) QL22. The team engaged this force resulting in 24 NVA KBH and 10 VC KBH.

Also on the 18th, E/1-9 engaged another large group of NVA in the Iron Triangle area. The Blues were not inserted and the Brigade, due to a lack of assets, was unable to react to this contact. E/1-9 engaged with organics, artillery and AFA with unknown results. Several personnel were wounded and the Troop had another LOH destroyed during the contact.

2. Task Organization: As of 18 January 1971

BDE. CONTROL	TF 1-9	TF 3-17
D/1-9	A/1-9	B/3-17
H Co. 75th Rangers	A/3-17	B/1-9
62nd Inf. Plt. CTT	E/1-9	C/1-9
	D/3-17	
	F/1-9	

3. Intelligence Summary:

No change

4. Activities Statistics:

a. Airmobile Operations Insertions Extractions
   Ranger Teams   6   5
   CTT Teams   4   4
   Blues   15   15

b. Aircraft Firings HIT NOT HIT CRASHED/DESTROYED
   A/1-9   0   1
   C/1-9   1   1
   E/1-9   2   1
   B/3-17   1   0   1

c. Friendly Losses   Enemy Losses
   KIA   0   KBH   34
   WIA   4   KIA   1
   MIA   0   WIA   0
                           VCS   8
                           VCC   3
                           NVAC   0
                           KBAFA   0
                           KBARTY 0
                           KBAS   0

20-23 January 1971

1. Operations Summary:

During these four days there were 10 aircraft firings reported. Visual Reconnaissance continued as usual in the Division and ARVN AO with no significant contacts or findings made by the Brigade. C/1-9 and E/1-9 made several insertion and extraction sorties with the ARVN Browns and the American Rangers.

2. Task Organization:

No change

3. Intelligence Summary:

A POW captured at an ambush site on highway QL22 in Tay Ninh Province and documents taken from a KBH showed that anti-helicopter training is being stressed in the Cambodia Training Centers.

4. Activities Statistics:

a. Airmobile Operations	Insertions	Extractions
Ranger Teams	5	4
CTT Teams	2	2
Blues	16	16

b. Aircraft Firings	HIT	NOT HIT	CRASHED/DESTROYED
A/1-9	0	3	
C/1-9	1	1	
E/1-9	2	2	
F/1-9	0	2	

c. Friendly Losses   Enemy Losses
   KIA   1   KBH   5
   WIA   5   KIA   4
   MIA   0   WIA   0
                            VCS   2
                            VCC   1
                            NVAC   0
                            KBAFA   0
                            KBARTY 0
                            KBAS   0

24-31 January 1971

1. Operations Summary:

The last week of the month saw many ground to air firings and an indirect fire attack on Song Be accompanied with light small arms fire from outside the perimeter.

The most notable incident of the 8 day period was the contact in which Air Cavalry assets supported the 6th ARVN Ranger Group. The ARVN's were committed to an all-day contact with an estimated company of the enemy. At 1115 hours both an AH-1G and OH-58 from A/3-17 received ground to air fire with negative hits or injuries. Enemy locations were engaged with organics and a section of AFA, with negative assessments. At 1255 hours another section of AFA was committed and at 1335, a third section was bounced. The friendlies were in a small bomb crater in dense forest, receiving heavy enemy fire. A/3-17, C/1-9 and E/1-9 provided continuous support. The enemy inflicted heavy casualties on the friendlies. Out of 52 ARVN's and 3 US advisors, only 11 ARVN and 1 US advisor were able to function effectively. A relief force was accidentally engaged by the Republic of Vietnam Air Force. At 1505 hours, the American advisor said that contact was broken; however, 1000 meters from the friendlies the relief force came under intense enemy fire, at 1630 hours. A/3-17 and AFA supported the relief element. At 1730 hours contact was broken and at 1910 hours all medevacs were completed. The lesson learned here is:

When US Air Cavalry or US Air Force support ARVN ground forces, an American Advisor must be with them on the ground. Also, either USAF or RVAF be used, but not both, unless radio contact is established with the RVAF aircraft.

2. Task Organization:

No change

3. Intelligence Summary:

No change

4. Activities Statistics:

a. Airmobile Operations   Insertions   Extractions
   Ranger Teams   11   14
   CTT Teams   4   4
   Blues   42   42

b. Aircraft Firings HIT   NOT HIT   CRASHED/DESTROYED
   A/1-9   1   2
   B/1-9   0   2
   C/1-9   1   0
   E/1-9   0   2
   F/1-9   2   8   1
   A/3-17   4   4   1
   B/3-17   0   2

c. Friendly Losses   Enemy Losses
   KIA   1   KBH   22
   WIA   5   KIA   5
   MIA   0   WIA   0
                           VCS   0
                           VCC   0
                           NVAC   0
                           KBAFA   0
                           KBARTY   0
                           KBAS   0

Note: A/3-17 found 5 NVA bodies of an earlier contact. They found papers on the bodies that confirmed the presence of the 101st NVA Regiment in the AO.

3 new Forward Support Bases were opened in the AO.

**This Map shows the Stationing of
Air Cavalry assets from 1 of February through 15 February 1971**

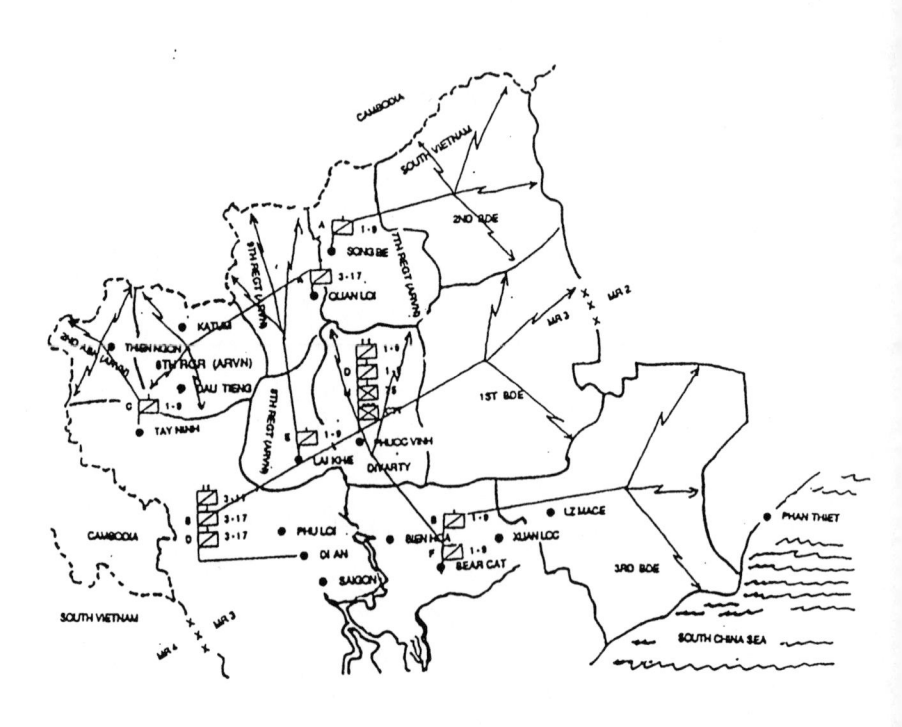

1 - 15 February 1971

1. Operations Summary:

During this period A/3-17, C/1-9 and Ranger operations highlighted the period. Ranger Teams had contact on three (3) separate occasions, resulting in 11 enemy KIA. As a result of these contacts the Rangers captured 5 automatic weapons and 5 rucksacks.

C/1-9 operations with the 18th ARVN Division were experiencing coordination difficulties. On 7 February C Troop inserted their Blues to conduct ground reconnaissance. They established contact with an unknown size enemy force. After considerable delay in locating the designated ARVN QRF, the QRF was inserted into the contact area. Once these forces were joined they moved forward again and re-established contact with the enemy force. At this time the RRF was requested and the 52nd ARVN Regiment was informed that once the RRF was on the ground the Blues would be extracted. The 52nd Regiment refused to commit the RRF unless the Blues stayed on the ground. To prevent possible loss of troops while this was being resolved the Blues and QRF were extracted.

On 13 February a C Troop Scout received ground to air fire from 2 locations. The area was engaged with organics and artillery. At 1045 hours the Scout received more ground to air fire and also observed two .51 calibre anti-aircraft positions. In one of the positions he observed an unmanned .51 calibre machine gun. At 1115 hours the Scout detected another .51 calibre machine gun. The 52nd Regiment was contacted to put a force into the area. They refused to go until after our Blues were inserted. At 1200 hours C Troop requested a QRF from the Brigade. A/3-17 Blues were designated as the QRF and placed on standby. At 1400 hours C Troop Blues were inserted and followed a trail to a small bunker complex which had been used that day. They continued reconnaissance in the area, locating a .51 calibre position with no weapon. At 1500 hours the Blues established contact with an unknown size enemy force and requested that the QRF be inserted. At 1530 hours the QRF was inserted and linked up with C Troop Blues. As they continued their reconnaissance they heard movement all around them. The Troop Commander requested that the

ARVN RRF be inserted into the area. The Troop Commander was informed that there would be no RRF forthcoming unless he could assure the ARVN Commander or the US Advisors that the RRF could be extracted before dark. Since the Troop Commander could not give such assurance, he moved the QRF and the Blues back to a PZ and extracted them.

On 15 February at 1300 hours A/3-17 Pink Team located four 6 X 6 bunkers with evidence of recent use. At 1535 hours the Blues were inserted and located a large rice cache consisting of 100, 200 pound sacks of rice. These bags of rice were stacked in piles of 30 sacks per pile. Conducting reconnaissance in the vicinity of the cache the Blues located a bunker complex and were in contact with an unknown size enemy force. At 1610 hours an OH-58 was shot down supporting the contact. The crew was extracted and AFA and a Medevac were requested. Contact with the enemy continued and the Blues suffered 1 Kit Carson Scout KIA and four Blues WIA. At 1625 hours an ARVN QRF was inserted and during the insertion the Troop Commander, in an OH-58, was shot down. He and the crew were extracted. At 1630 hours A/3-17 requested more support from Brigade and E/1-9 was directed to provide 3 Pink Teams and their Blues. At 1645 hours a Cobra was hit with ground to air fire with negative injuries. By 1745 hours a total of 6 Blues were WIA and 2 KIA. At this time the Troop Commander called for the ARVN RRF but they were unable to provide one due to a heavy contact they were involved in. The Troop Commander then moved the Blues and the QRF back to a PZ. By 1800 hours all forces had been extracted. Artillery was adjusted on the area and fired throughout the night. The ARVN's were unable to conduct operations in the area until the 17th of the month, at which time they evacuated or destroyed all the rice.

At 1100 hours on the 15th, C/1-9 observed and killed an individual in a bunker. Another one was located but evaded the area. Artillery was requested and destroyed six of the eight bunkers that had been observed. The Troop Commander requested a QRF and a RRF prior to the insertion of the Blues to conduct ground reconnaissance. The 52nd Regiment conditionally provided them with the understanding that they would not go in unless the Blues remained on the ground. The Troop Commander inserted the Blues to conduct ground reconnaissance. There were no significant findings except for one recently prepared position in the area. The Troop Commander believed that what the Troop located were positions prepared by an advance party for a larger group.

The problem with the 52nd Regiment is getting resolved slowly. The basic problem is a lack of understanding on the part of the US advisors and the ARVN Regiment on the employment principles of Air Cavalry. Not having worked with Air Cavalry before, they are reluctant to commit forces to contacts established by Air Cavalry. This problem will be overcome as they gain more confidence and a better understanding of Air Cavalry tactics and techniques.

2. Task Organization:

No change

3. Intelligence Summary:

No change

4. Activities Statistics:

a. Airmobile Operations

	Insertions	Extractions
Ranger Teams	29	25
CTT Teams	0	0
Blues	65	65

b. Aircraft Firings

	HIT	NOT HIT	CRASHED/DESTROYED
A/1-9	0	5	
B/1-9	1	4	
C/1-9	1	3	
E/1-9	3	3	1
F/1-9	2	3	
A/3-17	2	0	1
B/3-17	0	2	

c. Friendly Losses   Enemy Losses
   KIA   2[6]   KBH   12
   WIA   11   KIA   13
   MIA   0   WIA   6
                            VCS   0
                            VCC   0
                            NVAC   1
                            KBAFA   1
                            KBARTY 0
                            KBAS   0

---

[6] Note: includes 1 KCS assigned to A/3 - 17.

TAB A

9TH AIR CAVALRY BRIGADE (PROVISIONAL)

COMBAT AFTER ACTION REPORT
1 SEPTEMBER 1970 - 15 FEBRUARY 1971

DECISION PAPER
23 AUGUST 1970

1ST CAVALRY DIVISION (AIRMOBILE)
PHUOC VINH, SOUTH VIETNAM

AVDACT-DT

Course of Action to provide additional VR capabilities within 1 ACD AO.

1. C of S   Approve__   Disapprove__
   ADC-B   Approve__   Disapprove__
   CG   Approve__   Disapprove__

2. This is a decision paper.

3. Problem:

    How to obtain additional VR capabilities, from organic 1 ACD organic assets, in the FIRST TEAM AO.

4. General:

    a. A conference was held by BG Burton; ADC-B, on 220930 August, 1 ACD to present and discuss feasible courses of action and arrive at a recommended solution to the problem of how to best obtain additional VR capabilities in the 1 ACD AO.

    b. The following persons were present at the conference and provided their comments and expertise on the courses of action presented and the final recommendation.

(1) BG Burton, J.R.	ADC-B, 1ACD
(2) COL Meyer, E.C.	Chief of Staff
(3) COL Brady, M.J.	CO, DIVARTY
(4) COL Hamlet, J.R.	CO, 11th CAG
(5) LTC Martin, G.P.	ADAO
(6) LTC Toepel, A.E.	CO, 2-20 ARA
(7) LTC Toner, F.B.	CO, 15th TC
(8) LTC Nevins, R.H.	CO, 1-9 CAV
(9) MAJ Soltes, C.R.	AC of S, G4, Aircraft Maint
(10) MAJ Armstrong, C.	AC of S, G3 D&T
(11) MAJ Chewning, W.M.	AC of S, G3 D&T

AVDACT   23 August 1970

SUBJECT: Courses of Action to provide additional VR capabilities within 1 ACD AO.

5. Discussion:

The following courses of action were presented and discussed:

   a. 1st Course of Action: Formation of a Brigade Heavy Air Cavalry Platoon (Provisional). (Inclosure 1)

   b. 2nd Course of Action: Pool Division LOH assets and combine with AH-1Gs from D Co 227 or D Co 229 to form Pink Teams. (Inclosure 2)

   c. 3rd Course of Action: Reinforce A, B and C Troops of 1-9 Cav. (Inclosure 3)

   d. 4th Course of Action: Organize a fourth and fifth Air Cav Troops in 1-9 Cav. (Inclosure 4)

6. Recommendation:

   a. That Course of Action #4; Organize a fourth and fifth Air Cav Troop in 1-9 Cav, be adopted in part as follows: Organize one (1) D Company (227th or 229th) as 'E' Troop 1-9 Cav (Provisional) on 25 August 1970.

7. Steps to be taken:

   a. Transfer four LOH aircraft from each Brigade Aviation Platoon and reassign these aircraft to the new 'E' Troop 1-9 Cav (Provisional) with crew.

   b. Augment the DS Maintenance detachment of the selected 'D' Company 227 or 229 with the capability to maintain 12 LOH aircraft.

   c. Infuse sufficient 1-9 Cav aviators into the new 'E' Troop 1-9 to provide a training base.

d. 1-9 Cav prepare the required MTOE documents for 'E' Troop 1-9 Cav (Provisional) for submission to AC of S, G3.

8. Factors to be analyzed prior to forming a second Troop: F Troop 1-9 Cav.

a. Is there a requirement/need for an Aero Rifle Platoon in the two additional Air Cav Troops? If so should a Platoon from D\1-9 be considered to fill this requirement?

b. Is there a requirement to have organic UH-1H lift ships in the E & F Troops of 1-9 Cav to insert and extract the Aero Rifle Platoons if they are required.

4 Incls
as

/s/ Ward N. Chewning, Jr.
/t/ WARD N. CHEWNING, JR.
Major, GS
AC of S, G3 D & T

Inclosure 1 (Course of Action 1), to Decision Paper.

1st Course of Action: Formation of a Brigade heavy air cavalry platoon.

1. Mission:

To provide organic VR capability/mission for the brigade.

2. Concept:

a. The Heavy Air Cavalry Platoon (provisional) would be an organic unit within each Brigade under the Brigade Commander's Command and Control. It would be designed to provide the necessary VR capability for the Brigade AO. This concept will allow the 1-9 Cav to have the ability to concentrate throughout the 1 ACD AO as necessary.

b. The Heavy Air Cavalry Platoon would consist of the following assets:

(1) The Brigade Aviation Platoon as a nucleus to build upon.

(2) A minimum of 6 AH-1G aircraft; preferably 8 AH-1G aircraft, from D Cos 227 and 229 to pair with the eight (8) LOH within the Brigade Aviation Platoon thereby forming Pink Teams. 1-9 Cav would provide the expertise in the form of experienced Pink Team aviators.

(3) A provisional reconnaissance platoon with capabilities similar to the 1-9 Cav 'Blue' platoon.

3. Advantages:

a. The Brigade Commander would have his own organic VR capability immediately at hand under his own control.

b. The 1-9 Cav would be relieved of the responsibility for furnishing all the VR capability within the Brigade AO. Therefore gaining greater flexibility to concentrate on specific areas within the 1 ACD AO. This would not prevent the 1-9 Cav from reinforcing the VR capability of each brigade.

4. Disadvantages:

a. MTOE action would have to be initiated in numerous units; examples of this follow.

(1) Deletion of D Co's of 227 and 229 to include the HQ's elements.

(2) MTOE action to enlarge the brigade aviation platoons to include the immediate requirement for the forming of 3 DS maintenance detachments.

(3) MTOE action to form the provisional reconnaissance platoon. The troops would have to come from 1 ACD (brigade) assets.

b. Lift ships assets would have to be provided either by providing organic, dedicated or standby aircraft for the insertion and extraction of the reconnaissance platoon.

c. Both the brigade Pink Teams and the reconnaissance platoon would require extensive training before they would be an efficient organization.

d. The 2-20 ARA would be tasked to provide both gun-ship cover and continue its ARA mission.

Inclosure 2 (Course of Action 2), to Decision Paper.

2nd Course of Action: Pool Division LOH assets and combine with AH-1 Gs from Co's D-227 or D-229 to form Pink Teams.

1. Mission:

To provide V/R within each Brigade AO.

2. Concept:

   a. This course of action envisions the combination of AH-1G's from D Co 227th or D Co 229th with the LOH aircraft of the division and each Brigade Aviation Platoon, if necessary, to form 3 to 4 Pink Teams for each Brigade who would conduct VR within the respective Brigade AO on a mission basis. At the end of the day's missions all aircraft would return to their respective units.

   b. Each Brigade would assign missions and control the VR within its respective AO.

   c. Each Brigade would utilize its QRF Platoon to follow up on intelligence gathered and contacts made by these Pink Teams.

   d. 1-9 Cav would continue to conduct VR within the three Brigades AO at a reduced level while freeing more 1-9 Cav assets to concentrate on other special areas.

3. Advantages:

   a. There would be no requirements to initiate TOE or MTOE action.

   b. D Co 227 and D Co 229 would retain their maintenance capabilities and could continue to perform limited gun-ship cover for lift ships.

   c. 2-20 ARA would not be required to furnish all the gun-ship cover required for the lift ships.

d. This concept would provide the required amount VR for each Brigade, under Brigade control, while freeing 1-9 Cav to either reinforce all or one particular Brigade or work in a separate AO.

4. Disadvantages:

a. The Pink Teams that would be formed would not have the expertise of those in the 1-9 Cav and would reqreui extensive training.

b. The Brigade QRF would not have the expertise or normal organic aircraft support that the 1-9 Cav 'Blues' have.

Inclosure 3 (Course of Action 3) to Decision Paper.

3rd Course of Action: Reinforce A, B and C Troops of 1-9 Cav.

1. Mission:

Provide normal VR for each Brigade within the 1 ACD AO.

2. Concept:

Provide 1-9 Cav with additional Pink Team assets to enable it to provide greater VR throughout the 1 ACD AO. This concept will be accomplished by the expaionsn of all three Air Cav Troops of 1-9 Cav with AH-1Gs from D Co 227th and D Co 229th and with LOHs from each Brigade Aviation Platoon.

    a. The AH-1G and LOH assets will come from the following units in the following amount:

    (1) AH-1G aircraft: 6 from D-227 and 6 from D-229, with aviators.

    (2) LOH Aircraft: 4 from each Brigade Aviation Platoon, with aviators.

    b. 1-9 Cav with this expanded VR capability will be able to provide the normal VR requirements within each Brigade AO while having the capability to provide additional Pink Teams where needed.

3. Advantages:

    a. This concept would provide 12 additional Pink Teams, 4 teams for each Air Cav Troop, facilitating greater VR capability.

    b. 1-9 Cav could absorb the training requirement which would be necessary to train the new aviators in Pink Team tactics and techniques.

    c. This concept would not require the forming of additional DS maintenance detachments to maintain the additional 12 AH-1Gs and 12 LOH's. The current DS Maintenance Detachments could be augmented with personnel, equipment and PLL sufficiently to maintain the additional aircraft.

d. There would not be a requirement to form an additional 'Blue' Platoon.

e. The D Co's of the 227th and 229th would retain their identity with each having one half of their normal gun cover capability. The gun cover capability lost by D-227 and D-229 could be covered by 2-20 ARA with ease.

f. This version facilitates an easy transition back to the original concept/organization when desired.

4. Disadvantages:

a. The gun cover capability of D-227 and D-229 would be cut in half.

b. 2-20 ARA would be required to execute gun cover missions in addition to ARA type missions.

c. HQ's elements of D-227 and D-229 would be administratively top heavy.

Inclosure 4 (Course of Action 4) to Decision Paper.

4th Course of Action: Organize a fourth and fifth Air Cav Troop in 1-9 Cav.

1. Mission:

To provide additional VR capability within the 1 ACD AO.

2. Concept:

Utilize 'D' Companies of 227 and 229 to form a nucleus for the organizing of E Troop 1-9 Cav and F Troop 1-9 Cav. This concept would provide the maximum number of Pink Teams within the 1 ACD. The 12 LOH aircraft located in the Brigade Aviation Platoons would be drawn and distributed evenly between D-227 and D-229. Each Brigade would be tasked to have a standby QRF to be utilized to follow up the findings of these two new troops. 2-20 ARA will assume all gun cover missions and ARA missions. DS Maintenance Detachments of D-227 and D-229 will be augmented with sufficient mechanics and equipment to maintain the LOH aircraft.

3. Advantages:

    a. The basic organization of D-227 and D-229 will be maintained.

    b. Maximum additional VR capability will be obtained.

    c. 1-9 Cav will be able to infuse experienced Pink Team Aviators within the new troops with ease. In addition, 1-9 Cav will have sufficient assets in Pink Teams to concentrate/saturate the 1 ACD AO with VR.

4. Disadvantages:

    a. Brigade Aviation Platoons will lose their LOH aircraft.

    b. 2-20 ARA will have to assume the mission of gun cover and ARA entirely.

c. MTOE action will have to be initiated for all units involved such as D-227, D-229, 1-9 Cav and the Brigade Aviation Platoons.

d. LOH mechanics and PLL will be required in the DS Maintenance Detachments of the two new troops.

e. The two new troops will not have organic 'Blue' Platoons as does A, B and C Troops of 1-9 Cav.

TAB B

9TH AIR CAVALRY BRIGADE (PROVISIONAL)

COMBAT AFTER ACTION REPORT
1 SEPTEMBER 1970 - 15 FEBRUARY 1971

INFORMATION PAPER TO G3 ON FORMING
PROVISIONAL TROOP
24 AUGUST 1970

1ST CAVALRY DIVISION (AIRMOBILE)
PHUOC VINH, SOUTH VIETNAM

DEPARTMENT OF THE ARMY
HEADQUARTERS, 1ST SQUADRON (AIRMOBILE) 9TH CAVALRY
1ST CAVALRY DIVISION (AIRMOBILE)
APO San Francisco 96490

AVDARS-3   24 August 1970

SUBJECT: Increased VR Capabilities of 1st Squadron, 9th Cavalry within 1 ACD AO.

Commanding General
ATTN: G3 D & T
1st Air Cavalry Division APO San Francisco 96490

1. The following information is provided to complement the staff study dated 23 August 1970, HQ 1 ACD, Subject: 'Courses of Action to provide additional VR capabilities within the 1 ACD AO.' Course of Action number four (4) was approved. This course of action recommends two (2) additional Air Cavalry Troops to be organized from current 1 ACD assets and assigned to the 1st Squadron, 9th Cavalry. Implementation will be phased, with the first Troop to be organized, on or about, 25 August 1970. Organization date of the second troop to be announced.

2. The data contained herein are the results of a comparison of the Tables of Organization for 'D' Co 227 or 229, AHB with the Air Cavalry Troop in the Air Cavalry Squadron.

3. This comparison reflects the requirements for the formation of the fourth Air Cavalry Troop. It assumes the utilization of one (1) platoon from 'D' Troop, 1st Squadron 9th Cavalry, as the organic rifle platoon. Formation of a fifth Air Cavalry Troop would require a rifle platoon from assets outside the 1st Squadron, 9th Cavalry.

/s/ Robert H, Nevins
/t/ ROBERT H. NEVINS
LTC AR
Commanding

* Author's Note: In the file copy I have access to, there was no cover sheet for the following comparisons.

INDEX

I. Comparison of personnel requirements for a new Air Cavalry Troop and the personnel of 'D' Company 227 or 229, one half the resources of the Brigade Aviation Sections and the selected resources of the 1st Squadron, 9th Cavalry.

II. Comparison of equipment requirements for a new Air Cavalry Troop and the equipment resources of 'D' Company 227 or 229, one half the resources of the Brigade Aviation Sections, and the selected resources of the 1st Squadron, 9th Cavalry.

III. Comparison of DS Maintenance Detachment personnel requirements for a new Air Cavalry Troop and the personnel resources of the DS Maintenance Detachments available in the selected 'D' Company of 227 or 229.

IV. Comparison of the maintenance equipment requirements for the DS maintenance Detachment for a new Air Cavalry Troop and the resources of the DS Maintenance from the selected 'D' Company of 227 or 229.

I

Comparison of personnel requirements for a new Air Cavalry Troop and the personnel of 'D' Company 227 or 229, one half the resources of the Brigade Aviation Sections and the selected resources of the 1st Squadron, 9th Cavalry.

The following is a list of minimum essential personnel and equipment which will be needed in addition to the assets of 'D' Company 227 or 229, Brigade Aviation Sections, 1-9 Air Cavalry Squadron, the DS Maintenance Detachments of 'D' companies of 227 or 229 and the 1-9 Air Cav. These minimum additional assets will enable the proposed 'E' Troop 1-9 Cavalry to perform the mission of an Air Cavalry Troop.

PERSONNEL - AIR CAVALRY TROOP

E-1	11D50	1
E-7	67Z50	1
E-6	67W2F	2
E-5	11D40	1
E-5	05C40	1
E-4	05B20	1
E-4	35K20	1
E-4	67V20	1
E-4	67N20	<u>1</u>
		10

PERSONNEL - DS MAINTENANCE DETACHMENT

E-5	35K20	1
E-5	35M20	1
E-5	44E20	1
E-5	67N20	3
E-5	67V20	2
E-5	68B20	1
E-5	68E20	1
E-4	35K20	1
E-4	67N20	4
E-4	67V20	2
E-4	68B20	<u>1</u>
		18

MTOE 17 - 097T0
Bde
D Avn N E

Par	Line No.	Description	Grade	MOS	BR	Req	D Co.	Avn Sec	N E 1-9D X *
01	01	Troop Commander	MAJ	61204	AR	1	1		
	02	Executive Officer	LT	61204	AR	1	1		
	03	Operations Officer	LT	61204	AR	1	1		
	04	Maint Officer	LT	61204	AR	1	1		
	05	LNO	LT	61204	AR	1	1		
	06	1SG	1SG	11D50		1			1
	07	Flt Op SGT	SFC	71P40		1	1		
	08	Supply Sgt	SGT	76Y40		1	1		
	09	Comm Chief	SGT	31G40		1			1
	10	Inf. Sgt	SGT	11D40		1			1
	11	RTT Operator	SGT	05C40		1			1
	12	Sr Rad Operator	SP4	05B20		1			1
	13	Troop Clerk	SP5	71H20		1	1		
	14	Op Clerk	SP4	71B20		1	3		2
	15	Supply Clerk	SP4	76Y20		2	3		1
	16	Lt Trk Driver	PFC	11D10		2			2
	17	Radio Operator	PFC	05B20		2			2
02	01	Sect Ldr	LT	61204	AR	1	1		
	02	Helicopter Pilot	WO	100B	AV	1	1		
	03	Crew Chief	SP5	67N2F		2		2	
	04	Door Gunner	SP4	67A1F		2		2	
03	01	Sec Chief	WO	67100	AV	1	1		
	02	Maint Supr	SFC	67Z50		1	1		
	03	Tech Insp	SP6	67W2F		1			1
	04	Helicopter Mechanic	SP5	67N20		1	1		
	04	Helicopter Mechanic	SP5	67V20		1	1		
	04	Helicopter Mechanic	SP5	67Y20		1			1
	05	Sr Acft Armorer	SP5	45J20		2	1		1
	06	Acft Armorer	SP4	45J20		1	2		1
	07	Parts Specialist	SP4	76T20		1			1

* ND needs Need; Ex menas Excess

MTOE 17 - 097T0

Par No.	Line	Description	Grade	MOS	BR	Req	Bde Co.	D Avn Sec 1-9D	N E X
	08	Avionics Mech	SP4	35K20		1		1	
	09	Equip Rpts Clerk	SP4	71T20		1		1	
	10	Wheel Veh. Mech	SP4	63B20		1		1	
	11	Lt Trk Driver	PFC	63A1	0	2		1	
	12	Hel Mechanic	SP4	67V20		2		2	
	13	Hel Mechanic	SP4	67Y20		2		2	
04	01	Plt Commander	CPT	61204	AR	1	1		
	02	Plt Sgt	PSG	11D4F		1		1	
05	01	Sec Commander	LT	61204	AR	2	2		
	02	Team Leader	LT	61204	AR	2	2		
	03	Helicopter Pilot	WID	100B	AV	4	4		
	04	Sct Obs	SSG	11D4F		2		2	
	05	Sct Obs	SSG	11D4F		6		6	
	06	Crew Chief	SP5	67V2F		10	12		2
06	01	Plt Commander	CPT	61204	AR	1	1		
	02	Plt Sgt	PSG	11B40		1		1	
	03	RTT Oper	PFC	11B10		2		2	
07	01	Sec Ldr	LT	61204	AR	1		1	
	02	Hel Pilot	WO	100B	AV	9	7	2	
	03	Crew Chief	SP5	67N2F		4		2	
	04	Door Gunner	SP4	67A1	F	5		3	
08	01	Sqd Ldr	SSG	11B40		4		4	
	02	Team Ldr	SGT	11B40		8		8	
	03	Grenadier	SP4	11B20		8		8	
	04	Sr Rifleman	SP4	11B20		8		8	
	05	Rifleman	PFC	11B10		8		8	

MTOE 17 - 097T0

Par No.	Line	Description	Grade	MOS	BR	Req	Bde D Co.	Avn Sec	N 1-9D	E X
09	01	Plt Commander	CPT	61204	AV	1	1			
	02	Plt Sgt	SFC	67Z50		1			1	
10	01	Sec Commander	LT	61204	AR	2			2	
	02	Team Leader	LT	61204	AR	2			2	
	03	Hel Pilot	WO	100B	AV	15		10	3	
	04	Crew Chief	SP5	67Y20		10	11		1	
	05	Door Gunner	SP4	67A1F		10			10	
		Comm Chief	SGT	36K40		1				
		Wireman	SP4	36K20		1				
		Wireman	PFC	36K20		1				
		Ammo Helper	PFC	55A10		5				
		Ammo Str Sp	SP4	55B20		3				
		Maint Sgt	SGT	63C40		1				
		UH1 Maint Sup	SFC	67N40		4				
		UH1 Maint Sup	SSG	67N40		1				
		UH1 Maint Sup	SGT	67N40		1				
		UH1 Tech Supply	SP6	67N3F		2				
		Maint Supervisor	MSG	67Z50		1				
		Clerk Typist	SP4	71B20		2				
		Petro Str Sp	SP4	76W20		3				
		Mess Sgt	SFC	94B40		1				
		First Cook	SP6	94B20		1				
		Cook	SP5	94B20		1				
		Cook	SP4	94B20		1				
		Cook Helper	PFC	94A10		1				

RECAP

GRADE	MOS	SHORT	OVER
LT	61204	5	
WO	100B		3
E8	11D50	1	
	67Z50		1
E7	11B40	1	
	11D4F	1	
	67N40	4	
	67N50	2	
	94B40		1
E6	11B40	4	
	11D4F	2	
	67N3F		2
	67N40		1
	67W2F	2	
	94B20		1
E5	05C40	1	
	11B40	8	
	11D40	1	
	11D4F	6	
	36K40		1
	45J20	1	
	63C40		1
	67N20	1	
	67N2F	3	
	67N40		1
	67V2F		2
	67Y20		1
	94B20		1
E4	05B20	1	
	11B20	16	
	35K20	1	
	36K20	1	
	55B20		3
	63B20		1
	67A1F	13	

175

GRADE	MOS	SHORT	OVER
	67V20	2	
	67Y20	2	
	71B20		2
	71P20	1	
	76Y20		2
	76W20		3
	94B20		1
E3	05B20	1	
	11B10	10	
	11D10	2	
	36K20		1
	55A10		1
	63A10	1	
	67A10	2	
	94A10		1

NOTE: Additional 5 mess personnel would have to be added to HHT 1-9.

II

Comparison of equipment requirements for a new Air Cavalry Troop and the equipment resources of 'D' Company 227 or 229, one half the resources of the Brigade Aviation Sections, and the selected resources of the 1st Squadron, 9th Cavalry.

TO&E EQUIPMENT SHORTAGE AND OVERAGE

LINE	DESCRIPTION	SHORT	OVER
A72260	Antenna Group RC-292	3	
A78151	Antenna Group AN/GRA 50	1	
A90117	Armament Subsystem M-23	4	
A90436	Armament Subsystem XM-28		1
B49272	Bayonet-Knife W/Scabbard M-7	44	
B67081	Binocular 6X30 Military Reticle	20	
B67218	BinocularX5 70 Military Reticle		8
06817	Cable Telephone WD - 1/TT DR8	7	
68719	Charger Battery PP-3420/U		3
E63317	Compass Magnetic Unmtd Lensatic	18	
E70811	Compressor Reciprocating	1	
F09390	Cookset Field 5 Man	18	
F84952	Container Spare Parts Assy X-4		1
F91627	Demo Set Explosive Non-Electrc	4	
F97915	Desk Field 2 Foldng Stools	3	
G04437	Detector Kit Chemical Agent VGH		4
21472	Dispenser Pump Hand 15 Gal	2	
H51377	Filler Unit Water Purification Knap Sk	4	
H73392	Flashlight Plastic 2 Cell Baton		2
J43918	Generator Set Gas Eng 1.5 KW AC	1	
J44055	Generator Set Gas Eng 1.5 KW DC Shk Mtd	1	
J46110	Generator Set Gas Eng 3 KW DC Shk-Skd Mtd	1	
J71304	Goggles Sun Wind Dust		75
K29660	Helicopter Attack AH-lG		1
K31795	Helicopter Utility UH-1H	4	
K37329	Hoist Chain Hand 1.5 Ton	1	
L44575	Launcher Grenade 40 MM	25	
L57699	Life Preserver Parachute	84	
L60318	Light Beacon MX-7031/TVY	3	
L61939	Light Ignition Timing 3 Lead	2	
L63994	Light Set Gen Illum 25 Outfit	1	
L64131	Light Set Marker Emergency	1	
L92386	Machine Gun 7.62MM Light Flexible		26
M02607	Maintenance Platform Man Adjust	2	
M75715	Mount Tripod MG 7.62MM	4	

LINE	DESCRIPTION	SHORT	OVER
M55650	Panel Marker Air Liaison VS-1 7/GVX	6	
N96741	Pistol Cal .45 Auto	36	
N97015	Pistol Pyrotechnc	6	
0610	Pump Centrif Gas Driven 100 GPM	1	
O33039	Radio Set AN/GRC-106 Mntd In Jeep	1	
O34214	Radio Set AN/GRC-1 25 Mntd In 3/4 Ton	1	
O37005	Radio Set AN/PRC-25	12	
O38119	Radio Set AN/PRC-47	2	
Q42092	Radio Set AN/VRC-10	3	
Q53926	Radio Set AN/VRC-46 Mtd In 3/4 Ton Trk	1	
Q55114	Radio Set AN/VRC-49	1	
Q55373	Radio Set AN/VRC-49 Mtd In 3/4 Ton Trk	1	
Q78282	Radio Set Control Grp AN/GRA-39	2	
Q78319	Reeling Machine Cable Hand RO-39		1
R91244	Revolver Cal .38 4 Inch Barrel		3
R94977	Rifle 5.56MM M-16	39	
S35741	Saw Chain Gas Driven 18 Inch	2	
T77451	Sling Net 5000 LB Rated Capacity	5	
T78273	Sling Endless 4 FT Long	8	
T78316	Sling Carrying Universal	19	
T728410	SLING ENDLESS 8 FT LONG	40	
T78547	Sling Endless 10000 LB Cap 4 Inches Long	4	
U81707	Switchboard Telephone Manual SB-22/PT	10	
U93477	Table Folding Legs Wood		10
V27271	Tarpaulin 17 X 12 FT	10	
V30252	Telephone Set TA-1/PT	7	
V31211	Telephone Set TA-312/PT		2
V48441	Tent Frame Type Maint	1	
V76519	Test Set Electronic Circut AN/GRM-55	1	
V88027	Test Set Radio AN/VRM-1	1	
V28757	Tool Kit General Use TE-33	5	
W30949	Tool Kit Aircraft Mechanic General	1	
W33004	Tool Kit Auto Mechanic Lt Wt		1
W37483	Tool Kit Electric Equipment TK-1 101/GSQ		2
W59034	Tool Set Aircraft Armament Repair		1
W59189	Tool Set Aircraft Maint Ambl OH-6A	1	
W95440	Trailer Cargo 1/4 Ton 2 Wheel	2	

LINE	DESCRIPTION	SHORT	OVER
W95537	Trailer Cargo 3/4 Ton 2 Wheel		7
X23227	Transporter Airmobile Hydraulic Lift		2
X39872	Truck Cargo 3/4 Ton W/Winch		7
X55627	Truck Platform Utility 1/2 Ton W/Winch		1
X60833	Truck Utility 1/4 Ton 4 X 4	1	
X65121	Trunk Locker Metal And Wood	1	
X65258	Trunk Locker Plywood	3	
X80759	Typewriter Portable		1
Y33342	Watch Wrist Grade	21	

NON - TO & E EQUIPMENT OVERAGE

LINE	DESCRIPTION	AMOUNT
A03210	ACC OUTFIT GAS FLD RANGE	1
Al 6715	ADDING MACHINE	2
B250662	BEACON LT WT PTRL 8-1 0 WATT	18
B50696	BEACON RADIO LT WT PTRL HRT2-A	3
D65002	CASE FIELD OFC MACHINE PLYWOOD	2
D65276	CASE FIELD OFC MACHINE PLYWOOD	1
E75085	COMPUTER AIR/NAV	29
E92841	CENTRI PRESS FILLING DRUM	1
F96640	PMPG ASST FLAM LIQ 50 GPM 5 HP	2
G68998	DRUM FABRIC CLBSBL WTR 250 GAL	1
H83817	FOOD CNTR INSL RECT 5 GAL	4
J95865	GUIDON NYLON - WOOL BLANK	1
K25342	IMMERSION HEATER	5
L14430	JACK PANELS VEST AIR GRD RECOG	6
L65775	LIGHT TRF AFLD W/2 FILTERS	1
P90591	PUMP ASSY LT WT 30-40 GPM	12
R14154	RANGE OUTFIT FIELD GAS	2
R75709	REPAIR KIT TENTAGE	1
U44003	STOVE GAS BURNER	16
V05712	TABLE OUTFIT FIELD 4 COMPLETE	4
V43229	WATCH STOP TYPE B	7
V49948	TENT KITCHEN FLYPROOF	1
W31634	TOOL KIT ARMORERS	1
W34648	TOOL KIT CARPENTER ENG	1
W98825	TRAILER 1 1/2 TON 2 WHEEL	2
X40009	TRK CARGO 2 1/2 TON 6 X 6	2
X57408	TRK TANK FUEL SVC 2 1/2 TON	1
X80074	TYPEWRITTER NON PTBL	1

EQUIPMENT RECAPITULATION

LIN	DESCRIPTION	CAV TRP	D CO.	BDE AVN SEC	1-9	ND EX
A72260	Antenna Group RC-292	6	3		3	
A78151	Antenna Group AN/GRA 50	1			1	
A90117	Armament Subsystem N123	8		4	4	
A90436	Armament Subsystem XM-28	9	10			1
B29464	Barber Kit W/Case	1	1			
B49272	Bayonet-Knife W/Scabbard M-7	173	93	20	16	44
B67081	Binocular 6X30 Military Reticle	20			20	
B67218	Binocular 7X50 Military Reticle	2	10			8
C52738	Cabinet Tool And Spare Parts 11DR	1				
C53286	Cabinet Tool And Spare Parts	1				
C68710	Cable Telephone WD-1/TT DR8	16	8		7	
D68719	Charger Battery PP-3420/U	1	4			3
E63317	Compass Magnetic Unmtd Lensatic	41	15	4	4	18
E70811	Compressor Reciprocating	1			1	
F09390	Cookset Field 5 Man	43	16		18	
F84952	Container Spare Parts Assy X-4	1	2			
F91627	Demo Set Explosive Non-Electric	4			4	
F97915	Desk Field 2 Folding Stools	2	5			3
G04437	Detector Kit Chemical Agent VGH	1	5			
G21472	Dispenser Pump Hand 15 Gal	2			2	
H51377	Filler Unit Water Purification	4			4	
H73392	Flashlight Plastic 2 Cell Baton	76	70	8		2
J43918	Generator Set Gas Eng 1.5KW AC	1			1	
J44055	Generator Set Gas Eng 1.5 KW DC	1			1	
J46110	Generator Set Gas Eng 3 DC	1			1	
J71304	Goggles Sun Wind Dust	18	93			75
K30645	Helicopter Obs OH-6	10		10		
K29660	Helicopter Attack AH4-1G	9	10			1
K31795	Helicopter Utility UH-1H	8			4	4
K37329	Hoist Chain Hand 1.5 Ton	1			1	
L01121	Inverter Vibrator PP-68/U	1	1			
L44575	Launcher Grenade 40 MM	34	5		4	25
L57699	Life Preserver Parachute	186	102		84	

182

EQUIPMENT RECAPITULATION

LIN	DESCRIPTION	CAV TRP	D CO.	BDE AVN SEC	1-9	ND	EX
L60318	Light Beacon MX-7031/TVY	3			3		
L61939	Light Ignition Timing 3 Lead	2			2		
L63994	Light Set Gen Illum 25 Outfit	1	2				1
L64131	Light Set Marker Emergency	3	2		1		
L92386	Machine Gun 7.62MM Light Flexible	26			26		
M02607	Maintenance Platform Man Adjust	2			2		
M75715	Mount Tripod MG 7.62MM	4			4		
M55650	Panj El Marker Air Liason VS-17/GVX	14	8		6		
N96741	Pistol Cal .45 Auto	45	5		4	36	
N97015	Pistol Pyrotechnic	7	1		6		
P90610	Pump Centrif Gas Driven 100 GPM	1			1		
O33039	Radio Set AN/GRC-1 06 Mntd In Jeep	1			1		
O034214	Radio Set AN/GRC-1 25 Mntd 3/4 Ton	1			1		
O37005	Radio Set AN/PRC-25	18	6			12	
O38119	Radio Set AN/PRC-47	2			2		
O42092	Radio Set AN/VRC-10	27	10	10	4	3	
Q50754	Radio Set AN/VRC-24 Mtd 3/4 Ton	1			1		
Q53926	Radio Set AN/VRC-46 Mtd In 1/4 Ton	3	2		1		
Q54618	Radio Set AN/VRC-47 Mtd In 1/4 TON	1	1				
Q55114	Radio Set AN/VRC-49	1			1		
Q55373	Radio Set AN/VRC-49 MTD	1			1		
Q78282	Radio Set Control Grp AN/GRA-39	5	3		2		
Q78319	Radio Set Control Grp AN/GRA-74	1			1		
R30662	Rec/Tran Control Grp ANGRA-6	1	1				
R59160	Reeling Machine Cable Hand RO-39	10	4		6		
R91244	Revolver Cal.38 4 Inch Barrel	56	41	10	8	3	
R94977	Rifle 5.56MM M-16	92	47		4	39	
S27405	Safe 2 Shelves 1 Drw Compts	1	1				
S35741	Saw Chain Gas Driven 18 Inch	2			2		
T77451	Sling Net 5000 LB Rated Capacity	5			5		
T78273	Sling Endless 4FT Long	8			8		
T78316	Sling Carrying Universal	25	6		19		
T728410	Sling Endless 8FT Long	40			40		

EQUIPMENT RECAPITULATION

LIN	DESCRIPTION	CAV TRP	BDE D CO.	AVN SEC	1-9	ND	EX
T78547	Sling Endless 10,000 LB Cap 4 Inches	10	6		4		
U81707	Switchboard Tele Man SB-22/PT	1	1				
U93477	Table Folding Legs Wood	4	14				10
V27271	Tarpaulin 17X12 FT	14	4		10		
V30252	Telephone Set TA-1/PT	7			7		
V48441	Tent Frame Type Maint	4	6				2
V48921	Tent Of Medium Lt Wt	1	1				
V49058	Tent Of Small Lt Wt	2	2				
V76108	Test Set Elect Tube TY-7/U	1	1				
V76519	Test Set Elec Circuit AN/GRM-55	1			1		
V88027	Test Set Radio AN/VRM-1	1			1		
W28757	Tool Kit General Use TE-33	8	3		5		
W30812	Tool Kit Aircraft Tech Insp	2	2				
W30949	Tool Kit Aircraft Mech General	30	15	10	4	1	1
W33004	Tool Kit Auto Mechanic LT WT	1	2				1
W37483	Tool Kit Electric Equip TK-101/GSQ	1	3				2
W59034	Tool Set Aircraft Armament Repair	4	5				1
W59189	Tool Set Aircraft Maint AMBL OH-6A	1	1				
W59203	Tool Set Aircraft Maint ABL UH-1	1	1				
W95440	Trailer Cargo 1/4 Ton 2 Wheel	4	11				7
W95537	Trailer Cargo 3/4 Ton 2 Wheel	2	3				1
X23227	Transporter Airmobile Hydr Lift	1	3				2
X39872	Truck Cargo 3/4 Ton W/Winch	4	11				7
X55627	Truck Plat Utility 1/2 Ton W/Winch	2	3				1
X60833	Truck Utility 1/4 Ton 4X4	4	3		1	1	
X65121	Trunk Locker Metal And Wood	1			1	1	
X65258	Trunk Locker Plywood	2	5				3
X80759	Type Writer Portable	4	3		1	1	
Y33342	Watch Wrist Grade II	21			21		

MTOE REVISION

(A) MTOE 55-570GP01
    166th Trans Det (D-227)
    571st Trans Det (D-229)

(B) MTOE 55-570GP05
    98th Trans Det (A/1-9)
    545th Trans Det (B/1-9)
    151st Trans Det (C/1-9)

Proposed adjustment of A (above) to comply with personnel and equipment authorized in B (above).

RECAPITULATION

DEFICITS	ASSETS Excess from D Co 227	1-9 cav	REQUIREMENTS
1 E8 67Z50	1 E8 67Z50		1
1 E5 35K20			1
1 E5 35M20			1
1 E5 44E20			1
3 E5 67Y20	1 E5 67Y20		2
4 E5 67N20	1 E5 67N40		3
4 E5 67V20	2 E5 67V2F		2
1 E5 68B20			1
1 E5 68E20			1
1 E5 76T20	1 E5 76T20		
1 E4 35K20			1
2 E4 67Y20			2
4 E4 67N20			4
2 E4 67V20			2
1 E4 68B20			1
2 E3 67A10			2
1 E3 68A10			1

MTOE 55 - 570G
CMD P00568
UIC WOR1AA

Aircraft Maintenance Team (166 TC Det.)

PAR	LIN	DESCRIPTION	GR	MOS	BR	REQ	166th	ND	EX
01	01	Det Commander	LT	64823	TC	1	1		
	02	Acft Repair Tech	WO	67100		1	1		
	03	Avn Elec Eq Supv	E7	35P40		1	1		
	04	Acft Repair Chief	E8	67Z50		1	0	1	
	05	Acft Repair Foreman	E7	67Z50		1	1		
	06	Tech Insp	E6	67W20		2	2		
	07	Sr Avionics Mech	E5	35K20		1	0	1	
	08	Avn Comm Eq Rpmn	E5	35L20		2	2		
	09	Avn Con Eq Rpmn	E5	35N20		1	0	1	
	10	Avn Nav Eq Rpmn	E5	35M20		2	1	1	
	11	Machinist	E5	44E20		2	1	1	
	12	Sr Ad Armn Rpmn	E5	45J20		1	1		
	13	Sr Helicopter Rpmn	E5	67Y20		4	1	3	
	14	Sr Helicopter Rpmn	E5	67N20		4	0	4	
	15	Sr Helicopter Rpmn	E5	67V20		4	0	4	
	16	Sr Eng Rpmn	E5	68B20		2	1	1	
	17	Sr Rotor Prop Rpmn	E5	68E20		2	1	1	
	18	Acft Instr Rpmn	E5	68F20		1	1		
	19	Air Frame Welder	E5	68G30		1	1		
	20	Sr Airframe Rpmn	E5	68G20		1	1		
	21	Acft Repair Parts Sp	E5	76T20		1	0	1	
	22	First Cook	E5	94B20		1	1		
	23	Avionics Mech	E4	35K20		1	0	1	
	24	Acft Armn Rpmn	E4	45J20		1	2		1
	25	Gp Pwr Gen Mech	E4	52B20		1	1		
	26	Whl Veh Rpmn	E4	64B20		1	1		
	27	Helicopter Rpmn	E4	67Y20		4	2	2	
	28	Helicopter Rpm	E4	67N20		4	0	4	
	29	Helicopter Rpm	E4	67V40		2	0	2	
	30	Eng Rpmn	E4	68B20		2	1	1	
	31	Pwr Train Rpmn	E4	68D20		1	1		

PAR LIN	DESCRIPTION	GR	MOS	BR REQ	166th	ND	EX
32	Rotor Prop Rpmn	E4	68E20	1	1		
33	Acft Elec Rpmn	E4	68F20	1	1		
34	Airframe Rpmn	E4	68G20	1	1		
35	Hyd Sys Rpmn	E4	68H20	1	1		
36	Det Clerk	E4	71H20	1	1		
37	Eq Record Clk	E4	71T20	1	1		
38	Acft Repair Parts Sp	E4	76T20	1	2		1
39	Comm Repair Parts SP	E4	76U20	1	1		
40	Hel Rpmn Appr	E3	67A10	2	0	2	
41	Tool Room Keeper	E3	68A10	2	1	1	
42	Supply Clerk	E3	76A10	1	1		

IV

Comparison of the maintenance equipment requirements for the DS maintenance Detachment for a new Air Cavalry Troop and the resources of the DS Maintenance from the selected 'D' Company of 227 or 229.

SHORTAGES AND OVERAGES
DS MAINTENANCE DETACHMENT
D COMPANY 227TH AHB

		SHORT	OVER
BA9272	Bayonet Knife	25	
C65276	Case Ofc Machine 34 1/2L	1	
E61584	Comparator Freq CM-77/USM		2
E84952	Parts Container X5	11	
F01197	Test Set AN/AIM-69		1
F09390	Cook Set	1	
F97915	Desk Field	1	
H40814	File Visible Index Book Unit	1	
H41020	File Visible Index Cabinet	1	
H42342	Filing Cabinet	1	
H73666	X Flashlight	20	
J43918	Gen Set Gas Eng 1.5 KW	1	
J47968	Gen Set Gas Eng 5 KW	1	
J71304	Goggles	11	
J95865	Guidon Blank Nyl	1	
M80242	Multimeter AN/USM - 223		1
N31327	Oscilloscope CS-8/U	1	
N72891	Paulen	6	
N96741	Pistol Cal .45	2	
R94799	Rifle 5.56mm M-16	25	
T78136	Sling Load Univ	3	
V4882	Tent GP Medium	3	
W34648	Tool Kit Mech Gen	20	
W43279	Tool Kit Electronic TK-105/G	1	
W48444	Tool Kit Eng & Pwr Trn Rpmn Acft	2	
Z68053	Tool Kit Radar and Radio Rpmn	1	
W95400	Tool Set Acft Armament Rpmn		1
X23227	Trk Cgo 1/2 Ton	1	
X39872	Transporter Ambl Hyd Lift	1	
X55627	Forklift Trk Hel Transport 3000lb.		2
X65121	Trunk Lockers	1	

MTOE 55-57OG

AIRCRAFT MAINTENANCE DETACHMENT EQUIPMENT

PAR	LIN	DESCRIPTION	REQ	166th	SEC	1-9	ND	EX
01	A58033	Analyser Spectrum TS-723/U	1	1				
	B15688	Bag Water	1	1				
	B29464	Barber Kit	1	1				
	BA9272	Bayonet Knife	63	38		25		
	C65002	Case Fld Ofc Mach 22 1/2 L	2	2				
	C65276	Case Fd Ofc Mach 34 1/2 L	2	1		1		
	E33083	Vac Cleaner	1	1				
	E61584	Comparator Freq CM-77/USM	N/A	2				2
	E63317	Compass	2	2				
	E75085	Computer Air Nav	2	2				
	E84952	Parts Container X5	13	2		11		
	F01197	Test Set AN/AIM-69	1	2				1
	F09390	Cook Set	2	1		1		
	F19198	Counter Electronic AN/USM-207	1	1				
	F97915	Desk Field	2	1		1		
	G21061	Dispensing Pump 12 Gal	1	1				
	G77126	Dummy Load Electrical DA-75/U	1	1				
	H01907	Elec Shop Mtd Avionics AN/ASM-146	2	2				
	H01912	Elec Shop Mtd Avionics AN/ASM-147	1	1				
	H40814	File Visible Index Book Unit	3	2		1		
	H41020	File Visible Index Cabinet	9	8		1		
	H42342	Filing Cabinet	7	6		1		
	H51915	Filter Separator Liquid Fuel 50 GPM	1	1				
	H73666	X Flashlight	40	20		20		
	H79221	Flood light Set Electric Portble	1	1				
	H83817	Food Container Insulated	3	3				
	J01004	Freq Motor AN/USM - 159	1	1				
	J36383	Gen Set Diesel 30KW PU - 406	2	2				
	J43918	Gen Set Gas Eng 1.5KW	2	1		1		
	J47968	Gen Set Gas Eng 5 KW	2	1		1		

PAR	LIN	DESCRIPTION	REQ	166th	SEC	1-9	ND	EX
	J49005	Gen Set Gas Eng 7.5 KW	1	1				
	J52495	Gen Sig AN/URM-25	1	1				
	J53682	Gen Sig AN/URM-103	1	1				
	J5371	Gen Sig AN/URM-127	1	1				
	J53782	Gen Sig AN/URM-44	1	1				
	J54330	Gen Sig 75 MEG Fixed Freq BC-376	1	1				
	J54741	Gen Sig SG-13/ARN	1	1				
	J55563	Gen Sig SG-297/U	1	1				
	J71304	Goggles	26	15		11		
	J95865	Guidon Blank Nyl	1	0				1
	K14403	Headset Electrical H-33/PT	2	2				
	K22581	Headset Microphone H-101/U	4	4				
	K23609	Headset Electrical H-216/U	1	1				
	L44575	Launcher Grenade 40mm	2	2				
	L63994	Light Set Gen III	1	1				
	L83824	Loud Speaker LS-215/U	1	1				
	L92386	MG 7.62mm M-60	2	2				
	M01100	Maint Kit MK-693A	2	2				
	M01374	Maint Kit Elec MK-722/ ARC-102	1	1				
	M01511	Maint Kit Elec MK-731/ ARC-51X	1	1				
	M01648	Maint Kit Elec MK-733/ ARC-54	1	1				
	M02036	Test Set MK-1035/ARC-131	1	1				
	M40157	Microphone Carbon M-29	1	1				
	M64001	Modulator Radio MK-83/ARN	1	1				
	M74714	Mount Tripod MG 7.62mm M-60	2	2				
	M80242	Multimeter AN/USM-223	9	8		1		
	M80276	Multimeter ME-30/U	1	1				
	M80413	Multimeter ME-26/U	1	1				
	M81783	Multimeter TS-585/U	1	1				
	M17155	Ohmmeter M-21A/U	1	1				
	N30572	Oscilloscope AN/USM-223	1	1				
	N31327	Oscilloscope CS-8/U	1	2				
	N722891	Paulen	10	4		6		
	N96741	Pistol Cal. 45	2	0		2		
	P06989	X Plotter Aircraft	2	2				
	P37218	Pwr Supply PP-1104/G	1	1				
	P96640	Pump Assy Flam Liq Blk Trf	1	1				

PAR	LIN	DESCRIPTION	REQ	166th	SEC 1-9	ND EX
	R75709	Repair Kit Tentage	1	1		
	R12444	Revolver Cal. 38	2	2		
	R94799	Rifle 5.56mm M-16	59	34	25	
	S58674	Screen Latrine	1	1		
	S69176	Shelter Ambl Acft Tool Sets	1	1		
	T17093	Shop Set A/C Maint UH-l/OH-6				
		CO Size Direct Supprt	1	1		
	T78136	Sling Load Univ	12	9	3	
	U23924	Steel Strapping & Sealing Kit	1	1		
	U44277	Stove Gas	2	2		
	U43299	Stopwatch	1	1		
	U93477	Table Fldg	4	4		
	V31211	Telephone Set TA-312/PT	4	4		
	V48441	Tent Maint Frame	2	2		
	V4882	Tent GP Medium	3	0	3	
	V52277	Tent Liner Frame Maint	2	2		
	V62066	Test Hamess Radio Set				
		AN/URM-157	1	1		
	V67203	Test Set TS-1588-AIC	1	1		
	V73847	Test Set Dir Finder AN/ARK493	1	1		
	V76103	Test Set Electron Tube TV-7/U	1	1		
	V84876	Test Set Radar AN/ARN-5	1	1		
	V86383	Test Set Radar AN/URM-98A	1	1		
	V87201	Test Set Radio AN/ARM-64	1	1		
	V88027	Test Set Radio AN/VRN-1	1	1		
	V91178	Test Set Radio Freq Pwr				
		AN/URM-120	1	1		
	V91863	Test Set Receiver AN/ARM-92	1	1		
	V99416	Test Set Resolver AN/ASM-101	1	1		
	W30675	Test Set Semi Conductor				
		TS-1836/U	1	1		
	W30812	Test Set Radar AN/ARM-239	1	1		
	W30949	Kit Airframe Repair	2	2		
	W33004	Tool Kit Aircraft Insp Technician	2	2		
	W34648	Tool Kit Mech Gen	23	3	20	
	W36703	Tool Kit Auto Mech Lt Wt	1	1		
	W37251	Tool Kit Carpenter Eng Sqd	1	1		
	W37388	Tool Kit Elec Rpmn Army Std	2	2		

PAR	LIN	DESCRIPTION	REQ	166th	SEC	1-9	ND	EX
	W39073	Tool Kit TK/100G	4	4				
	W43279	Tool Kit Electronic TK-105/G	1	0		1		
	W48444	Tool Kit Eng & Pwr Trn Rpmn Acft	5	3		2		
	W49681	Tool Kit Hvd Rpmn Acft	1	1				
	W59034	Tool Kit Prop & Rotor Rpmn Army Acft	2	2				
	Z68053	Tool Kit Radar and Radio Rpmn	2	1		1		
	W95400	Tool Set Acft Armament Rpmn	2	3				1
	W95537	Tool Set Acft Armament Rpmn Sup	1	1				
	X23227	Trk Cgo 1/4 ton 2 wheel	2	1		1		
	X39872	Transporter Ambl Hyd Lift	3	2		1		
	X52818	Trk Cargo T 4X4 w/winch	7	7				
	X55627	Forklift Trk Hel Transport 3000lb	3	5				2
	X60833	Trk Platform 1/2 ton 4X4 Mule	1	1				
	X63299	Trk Wrecker 5 Ton	2	2				
	X65121	Trunk Lockers	2	1		1		
	X80074	Typewriter Nonptbl 13"	1	1				
	X80348	Typewriter Nonptbl 20"	1	1				

TAB C

9TH AIR CAVALRY BRIGADE (PROVISIONAL)

COMBAT AFTER ACTION REPORT
1 SEPTEMBER 1970 - 15 FEBRUARY 1971

GENERAL ORDER FORMING E TROOP
11 DECEMBER 1970

1ST CAVALRY DIVISION (AIRMOBILE)
PHUOC VINH, SOUTH VIETNAM

DEPARTMENT OF THE ARMY
HEADQUARTERS, 1st CAVALRY DIVISION (AIRMOBILE)
APO San Francisco 96490

GENERAL ORDERS
NUMBER 21504   11 December 1970
TC 001. Following action directed.
E TROOP (PROVISIONAL), 1st SQUADRON 9TH CAVALRY
APO San Francisco 96490

Action: Organize

Asgd to: 1st Squadron, 9th Cavalry

Mission: To perform reconnaissance and provide security for combat elements and to engage in combat as an economy of force unit.

Effective date: VOCG, cfm 1 September 1970.

Authorized strength: Annex A.

Structure strength: N/A

Authority: VOCG, 1st Cav Div.

Special instructions: Personnel will remain assigned to parent organization and will be attached to E Troop (Provisional), 1st Squadron, 9th Cavalry for administration, rations, quarters and military justice. Promotion authority remains with the Commanding Officer of parent organization. Promotion will be effected against authorized position vacancies of parent unit.

FOR THE COMMANDER
OFFICIAL: G.E. NEWMAN
                                                       Colonel, GS
                                                       Chief of Staff

(s) Gordon E. Grant
(t) GORDON E. GRANT
    LTC, AGC
    Adjutant General

Annex A: Space Authorization for E Troop (Provisional)

DISTRIBUTION:
A Plus
5-ACofS, G3 D&T
10-1st Sqdn, 9th Cav

ANNEX A: (Space authorization for E Troop Provisional) to General Orders Number 21504

1. The following spaces are provided for E Troop (Provisional) except as indicated in paragraph c.

UNIT	MTOE	PARA	LINE	DESCRIPTION	GRADE	MOS	NUM
a. 1st Bde	67-42TP03	08	04	Rotary Wing Av	WO	100B0	4
2d Bde	(Each)		08	OH-6 Crew Chief	E5	67V20	4
b. 3rd Bde	67-42TP03	08	04	Rotary Wing Av	WO	100B0	2
			08	OH-6 Crew Chief	E5	67V20	2

c. D Co, 227th 1-1 57T ALL spaces except the following which are provided 2-20 Arty.

		04	01	Sect Commander	LT	01981	3
			02	Heli Pilot	WO	100E0	3
			03	AH-1G Crew Chief	E5	67N2F	3
d. 11thGS	1-102TP01	03	03	OH-6 Crew Chief	E5	67V20	2

e. 166th Trans 55-570GP01 All Spaces

f. HHT,1-9 Cav	17-96T	18	02	Heli Pilot	WO	100B0	2
		14	02	TI	E6	67W20	1
		18	03	Crew Chief	E5	67N20	2
		18	04	Door Gunner	E4	67A1	2
g. A,B, C Troop (each)		07	02	Heli Pilot	WO	100B0	2
		07	03	Crew Chief	E5	67N20	1
		07	02	Door Gunner	E4	67A1F	1

2. SUMMATION

LOSING UNIT	OFF	WO	EM
Bde's		10	10
D Co, 227th AHB	13	10	89
11th GS Co			2
1-9th Cav		8	11
166th Trans Det	1	1	36
TOTAL	14	29	148

TAB D

9TH AIR CAVALRY BRIGADE (PROVISIONAL)

COMBAT AFTER ACTION REPORT
1 SEPTEMBER 1970 - 15 FEBRUARY 1971

MANNING CHART FOR E TROOP

**1ST CAVALRY DIVISION (AIRMOBILE)
PHUOC VINH, SOUTH VIETNAM**

TYPE AIR CAVALRY TROOP

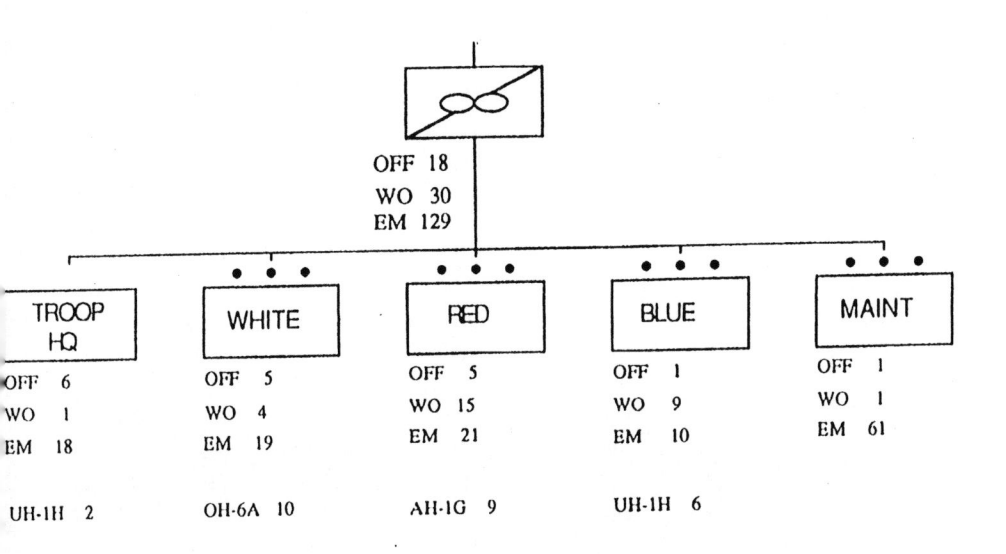

	TROOP HQ	WHITE	RED	BLUE	MAINT
OFF	6	5	5	1	1
WO	1	4	15	9	1
EM	18	19	21	10	61
	UH-1H 2	OH-6A 10	AH-1G 9	UH-1H 6	

Total: OFF 18, WO 30, EM 129

NOTES:

1. Troop Aviation Section is included with Troop Headquarters.
2. Current TOE utilizes UH-1C in Weapons (Red) Platoon
3. The Infantry Platoon is rotated on a ten day basis from D/1-9 Cavalry

AUTHORS NOTE:

In a typical Air Cavalry Troop the aggregate total for Enlisted Men would be 168 if the Rifle Platoon were added to the Blue Platoon as it is in a regular Air Cav Troop.

The Maintenance Section totals include the personnel from the 166th Maintenance Detachment.

MANNING

		AUTHORIZED			ASSIGNED			
PAR	LINE	GR	BR	MOS	GR	BR	MOS	FROM
TRP HQ								
01	01	MAJ	AR	61204	MAJ	AR	61204	1-9
	02	CPT	AR	61204	CPT	IN	71542	D-227
	03	LT	AR	61204	CPT	AR	61204	1-9
	04	LT	AR	61204	LT	-	64823	D-227
	05	LT	AR	61204	LT	-	1981	B/1-9
	06	1SG	NC	11D50	1SG		11D50	1-9
	07	SFC	NC	71P40	SFC		71P40	D-227
	08	SSG	NC	76Y40	SSG		76Y40	D-227
	09	SGT	NC	31Q40	SGT		31Q40	D-227
	10	SGT	NC	11D40	SP4		94L20	D-227
	11	SGT	NC	05B40	SP5		35H20	D-227
	12	SP4		05B20	SP4		71H20	D-227
	13	SP5		71H20	PFC		45M20	1-9
	14	SP4		71P20	SP4		36M20	D-227
	15	SP4		76Y20	PV2		76Al0	D-227
	16	PFC		11D10	SP4		36N20	D-227
	16	PFC		11D10	PFC		67Y20	D-227
	17	PFC		05B20	SP4		36K20	D-227
	17	PFC		05B20	SP5		68H20	D-227
AVN SEC								
02	01	LT	AR	61204	CPT	-	-	D-227
	02	WO	AV	100B	WO	AV	100B	C/1-9
	03	SP5		67N2F	SP4		-	
	03	SP5		67N2F	SP4		67N20	
	04	SP4		67AlF	SP4			
	04	SP4		67AlF	PFC		67Al0	
MAINT SEC								
03	01	WO	AV	6710	WO1	AV	100B	D-227
	02	SFC	NC	67Z50	SFC	NC	67M40	166
	03	SP6		67W2F	SP5		67W20	1-9
	03	SP6		67W2F	VACANT			
	04	SP5		67N20	SP5		67Y20	D-227

	AUTHORIZED				ASSIGNED		
PAR	LINE	GR	BR	MOS	GR BR	MOS	FROM
	04	SP5		67V20	SP4	67V20	D-227
	04	SP5		67Y20	SP5	67Y20	D-227
	05	SP5		45M20	E83	45M20	D-227
	06	SP4		45M20	SP4	45M20	D-227
	06	SP4		45M20	SP4	45M20	1-9
	07	SP4		76T20	VACANT		
	08	SP4		35M20	SP4	35K20	D-227
	09	SP4		71 T20	SP4	67Y20	D-227
	10	SP4		63B20	SP4	63B20	1-9
	11	PRD		63Al 0	SP4	55B20	D-227
	12	SP4		67V20	SP4	67Y20	D-227
	12	SP4		67V20	SP4	67Y20	D-227
	12	SP4		67Y20	SP4	67Y20	D-227
	12	SP4		67Y20	SP4	67Y20	D-227
	13	PFC		67Al 0	PFC	67Y20	D-227
	13	PFC		67Al 0	PFC	67Y20	D-227

SCOUT PLT HQ

04	01	CPT	AR	61204	CPT IN	61542	C/1-9
	02	PSG	NC	11D4F	SSG	-	1-9

1ST SCOUT SEC

05	01	LT	AR	61204	LT FA	1981	1-9
	02	LT	AR	61204	CW2 AV	100B	A/1-9
	03	WO	AV	100B	WO1 AV	100B	C/1-9
	03	WO	AV	100B	WO1 AV	100B	C/1-9
	04	SSG	NC	11D4F	SSG NC	11D40	1-9
	05	SGT	NC	11D4F	SGT NC	11D40	A/l-9
	05	SGT	NC	11D4F	SGT NC	67N20	3 BDE
	05	SGT	NC	11D4F	SP5	11D2F	C/1-9
	06	SP5		67V2F	SP4	67N20	2 BDE
	06	SP5		67V2F	SP4	67N20	3 BDE
	06	SP5		67V2F	PFC	67V20	1-9
	06	SP5		67V2F	SP4	67V20	1 BDE
	06	SP5		67V2F	VACANT		

		AUTHORIZED			ASSIGNED			
PAR	LINE	GR	BR	MOS	GR	BR	MOS	FROM

2ND SCOUT SECTION

PAR	LINE	GR	BR	MOS	GR	BR	MOS	FROM
05	01	LT	AR	61204	LT	-	1981	
	02	LT	AR	61204	CW2	AV	100B	
	03	WO	AV	100B	WO1	AV	100B	1 BDE
	03	WO	AV	100B	WO1	AV	100B	1 BDE
	04	SSG	NC	11D4F	SSG	NC	11D40	1-9
	05	SGT	NC	11D4F	SP4		11D40	C/1-9
	05	SGT	NC	11D4F	SP4		67V20	A/1-9
	05	SGT	NC	11D4F	SP4		67V20	A/1-9
	06	SP5		67V2F	SP4		67Y20	D-227
	06	SP5		67V2F	SP4		67N20	2 BDE
	06	SP5		67V2F	PFC		67V20	1-9
	06	SP5		67V2F	SP4		67V20	1-9
	06	SP5		67V2F	PFC		67AlO	C/1-9

RIFLE PLAT HQ

PAR	LINE	GR	BR	MOS	GR	BR	MOS	FROM
06	01	CPT	AR	61204	CPT	IN	1981	D-227
	02	PSG	NC	11B40	VACANT			
	03	PFC		11B10	VACANT			
	03	PFC		11B10	VACANT			

LIFT SEC

PAR	LINE	GR	BR	MOS	GR	BR	MOS	FROM
07	01	LT	AR	61204	CW2	AV	100B	A/1-9
	02	WO	AV	100B	CW2	AV	100B	1 BDE
	02	WO	AV	100B	WO1	AV	100B	B/1-9
	02	WO	AV	100B	WO1	AV	100B	1-9
	02	WO	AV	100B	WO1	AV	100B	B/1-9
	02	WO	AV	100B	WO1	AV	100B	1-9
	02	WO	AV	100B	WO1	AV	100B	D-227
	02	WO	AV	100B	VACANT			
	02	WO	AV	100B	VACANT			
	02	WO	AV	100B	VACANT			
	03	SP5		67N2F	SP4		67Y20	-
	03	SP5		67N2F	SP4		67Y20	-
	03	SP5		67N2F	SP5		67N20	-
	03	SP5		67N2F	VACANT			
	03	SP5		67N2F	VACANT			

	AUTHORIZED				ASSIGNED			
PAR	LINE	GR	BR	MOS	GR	BR	MOS	FROM
	04	SP4		67A1F	SP4		11B20	-
	04	SP4		67Al F	VACANT			
	04	SP4		67Al F	VACANT			
	04	SP4		67Al F	VACANT			
	04	SP4		67Al F	VACANT			

1ST RIFLE SQD

08	01	SSG	NC	11B40	VACANT
	02	SGT	NC	11B40	VACANT
	02	SGT	NC	11B40	VACANT
	03	SP4		11B20	VACANT
	03	SP4		11B20	VACANT
	04	SP4		11B20	VACANT
	04	SP4		11B20	VACANT
	05	PFC		11B10	VACANT
	05	PFC		11B10	VACANT

2ND RIFLE SQD

08	01	SSG	NC	11B40	VACANT
	02	SGT	NC	11B40	VACANT
	02	SGT	NC	11B40	VACANT
	03	SP4		11B20	VACANT
	03	SP4		11B20	VACANT
	04	SP4		11B20	VACANT
	04	SP4		11B20	VACANT
	05	PFC		11B10	VACANT
	05	PFC		11B10	VACANT

3RD RIFLE SQD

08	01	SSG	NC	11B40	VACANT
	02	SGT	NC	11B40	VACANT
	02	SGT	NC	11B40	VACANT
	03	SP4		11B20	VACANT
	03	SP4		11B20	VACANT
	04	SP4		11B20	VACANT
	04	SP4		11B20	VACANT
	05	PFC		11B10	VACANT

		AUTHORIZED			ASSIGNED			
PAR	LINE	GR	BR	MOS	GR	BR	MOS	FROM
	05	PFC		11B10	VACANT			

4TH RIFLE SQD

08	01	SSG	NC	11B40	VACANT			
	02	SSG	NC	11B40	VACANT			
	02	SSG	NC	11B40	VACANT			
	03	SP4		11B20	VACANT			
	03	SP4		11B20	VACANT			
	04	SP4		11B20	VACANT			
	04	SP4		11B20	VACANT			
	05	PFC		11B10	VACANT			
	05	PFC		11B10	VACANT			

WEAPONS PLATOON HQ

09	01	CPT	AR	61204	CPT	EN	1981	D-227
	02	PSG	NC	67Z50	SSG	NC	-	D-227

1ST WEAPONS SECT

10	01	LT	AR	61204	CPT	IN	61542	D-227
	02	LT	AR	61204	CW2	IN	61542	D-227
	03	WO	AV	100B	WO1	AV	100B	C/I-9
	03	WO	AV	100B	WO1	AV	100B	C/I-9
	03	WO	AV	100B	WO1	AV	100B	A/I-9
	03	WO	QV	100B	WO1	AV	100B	B/I-9
	03	WO	AV	100B	VACANT			
	03	WO	AV	100B	VACANT			
	04	SP5		67Y20	SP4		-	D-227
	04	SP5		67Y20	SP4		-	D-227
	04	SP5		67Y20	SP4		-	D-227
	04	SP5		67Y20	SP4		-	D-227
	04	SP5		67Y20	SP4		-	D-227
	05	SP4		67A1F	VACANT			
	05	SP4		67A1F	VACANT			
	05	SP4		67A1F	VACANT			
	05	SP4		67A1F	VACANT			
	05	SP4		67A1F	VACANT			

		AUTHORIZED			ASSIGNED			
PAR	LINE	GR	BR	MOS	GR	BR	MOS	FROM
10	01	LT	AR	61204	CPT	IN	1981	1-9
	02	LT	AR	61204	WO1	AV	100B	D-227
	03	WO	AV	100B	WO1	AV	100B	D-227
	03	WO	AV	100B	WO1	AV	100B	A/I-9
	03	WO	AV	100B	WO1	AV	100B	B/I-9
	03	WO	QV	100B	WO1	AV	100B	B/I-9
	03	WO	AV	100B	WO1	AV	100B	D-227
	03	WO	AV	100B	WO1	AV	100B	B/I-9
	03	WO	AV	100B	VACANT			
	03	WO	AV	100B	VACANT			
	04	SP5		67Y20	SP4		-	D-227
	04	SP5		67Y20	PFC		-	D-227
	04	SP5		67Y20	SP4		-	D-227
	04	SP5		67Y20	SP4		-	D-227
	04	SP5		67Y20	VACANT			
	05	SP4		67A1F	VACANT			
	05	SP4		67A1F	VACANT			
	05	SP4		67A1F	VACANT			
	05	SP4		67A1F	VACANT			
	05	SP4		67A1F	VACANT			

TOTAL AUTHORIZED: 18 OFF   30 WO   129 EM   177 AG

TAB E

9TH AIR CAVALRY BRIGADE (PROVISIONAL)

COMBAT AFTER ACTION REPORT
1 SEPTEMBER 1970 - 15 FEBRUARY 1971

LESSONS LEARNED IN FORMING A PROVISIONAL AIR CAV TROOP
20 OCTOBER 1970

1ST CAVALRY DIVISION (AIRMOBILE)
PHUOC VINH, SOUTH VIETNAM

DEPARTMENT OF THE ARMY
E TROOP 1ST SQUADRON 9TH (AIR) CAVALRY
1ST CAVALRY DIVISION (AIRMOBILE)
APO San Francisco 96490

AVDAAV-AH-X   20 October 1970

SUBJECT: Lessons Learned in forming a provisional Air Cavalry Troop

TO: Commanding Officer, 11th Aviation Group
    Commanding Officer, 1st Squadron 9th (Air) Cavalry

1. General: This report is intended to record the Lessons Learned in forming an Air Cavalry Troop from an existing aviation unit. Basically, there are four areas of interest that will be discussed; Equipment, Personnel, Maintenance and Training. Following a discussion of each area of interest I will conclude this report with the lessons learned.

2. EQUIPMENT:

   a. A listing of equipment shortages and equipment on hand is contained in enclosure one. This listing is based on what the Air Cavalry Troops in the Squadron are authorized by current TOE

   b. Receipt of equipment and reporting of equipment status has been an exercise in double book keeping. The Cobras, maintenance equipment, and maintenance facilities were carried on the 227th Assault Helicopter Battalion's (AHB) property books for a portion of the last month, then they were transferred to the 1-9 Cav Sqdn property books, and now they are to be returned to the 227 AHB property books and I am to sign hand receipts for this equipment. As far as the LOH's and UH-1H's are concerned, we have the same exercise contemplated. This will soon become an unmanageable situation as far as I am concerned. Every time I have a combat loss it means I will have to go through the unit on whose property book the aircraft is carried. This includes the 1st Sqdn 9th Cav, the 227th AHB and each Brigade in the Division. In addition to the above, it means I will have to report my equipment status to the organizations listed.

c. When the operational and maintenance aspects of this unit are separated into two separate and distinct categories, with the Troop reporting to different headquarters for each area, we have something less than a desirable situation. Inevitably one of the commanders in the chain of command is going to require that one of the areas take priority, and when that time arrives, this Troop, to use a colloquialism, will be between a rock and a hard place.

d. When the Troop was formed we were given one UH-1H, and were to receive the remaining lift helicopters at some time in the future. Being separated from the Squadron and our maintenance support by some distance, has required me to use this aircraft primarily as a maintenance aircraft. It was also incumbent upon me to train a lift section leader in anticipation of the receipt of the remaining aircraft. These two requirements were difficult to accomplish with just one UH-1H.

e. When I received the remaining aircraft (UH-1H) I only received four. This presently brings our total UH-1H aircraft in the Troop to five. This is not an adequate number of lift ships for me to effectively accomplish all aspects of my mission. I require a minimum of four aircraft to transport my Blue Platoon. I require one for a C&C aircraft, one for Maintenance, and a minimum of one additional aircraft so I can schedule maintenance properly.

f. In addition to the above, only two of the aircraft received had cargo hooks. This meant that one of these aircraft had to be used by maintenance to sling out damaged LOH'S. This affected my tactical operations somewhat, and has restricted my flexibility as far as scheduled maintenance is concerned. There have been days when I could only use two aircraft to insert my Blues. I have been fortunate to date in that this has not resulted in any losses due to employing my Blues piecemeal. When I was forced to use only two lift ships it has always meant a minimum of twenty minutes turn around, during which my two squads on the ground had to remain in the LZ to secure it for the last two lifts.

3. PERSONNEL:

   a. A listing of personnel assigned and my shortages are contained in enclosures two and three.[7] This listing is based on what the Air Cavalry Troops in the Squadron are authorized by current TOE.

   b. As with the equipment the assignment of personnel to this unit has posed some rather unique problems. The lack of a General Order designating this unit as a provisional unit has meant that the original personnel in D CO 227th AHB remained assigned to this unit. The remaining personnel we have received have been attached to the company in some cases and in other cases they have been assigned, by Division, to D CO 227th, AHB. In this situation it has been a prodigious task to determine who is actually assigned and who is attached. Many times we have received personnel who were assigned, on orders, to Troop E, 1-9 Cav Sqdn, which for morning report purposes does not exist.

   c. The lack of an organic 'Blue' Platoon has certainly created another unique situation. As originally conceived I was to have a Platoon from D Troop, 1-9 Cav, as a quick reaction force, to act as my Blue Platoon. They were to remain at Phouc Vinh with my lift (remaining) here at Lai Khe. This is an acceptable situation usually but when I have an aircraft go down in the southern part of the AO (as I did have), it takes entirely too long to get the Blues to the area of contact. In the situation just described it was faster to get one of the other Troops to insert their Blues. Although it was faster, it was not the desired solution.

   d. One other problem associated with this, and which should more properly be addressed in the training portion of this report, but which I will address here, is the fact that the Platoons from D Troop 1-9 Cav were rotated every ten days. This meant that I had to train each Platoon in the methods and procedures they were to use in conducting Airmobile operations (with E Troop).

---

[7] EDITORIAL NOTE: These enclosures are not included in this report.

e. One final comment on the personnel is the fact the Maintenance Detachment supporting the Troop was organized and equipped to support twelve Cobra aircraft. Upon receipt of the LOH's and UH-1H's there was no augmentation to the Maintenance Detachment. In addition, it would have been desirable to have received an LOH and UH-1H line chief and Technical Inspectors for these aircraft. If these personnel had been in the unit when the aircraft were received it would have simplified matters considerably.

4. MAINTENANCE:

a. The lack of an adequate number of maintenance personnel was the single most important factor affecting the maintenance within the Troop. Although the number and type of aircraft doubled, there was no increase in maintenance personnel.

b. Upon receipt of the LOH's it was found that eight of the twelve LOH's were below the maintenance standards of this Troop. This required an extra effort, at a critical period of time, to bring the aircraft up to standards. If our Troop had been given an opportunity to TI the aircraft prior to the Squadron accepting them, our work load would have been reduced substantially.

c. A more realistic issue of PLL for the LOH would have eased our initial problems with these aircraft. At the close of our first month of operation we had a 53% fill of our line items. This lack of spare parts seriously affected my OR (Operational Readiness) and MR (Mission Readiness) rate. At the present time I have achieved my highest fill to date, which is 73% of my basic load list.

d. Avionics equipment for the series three OH-6A has presented a continuing problem. There are no spare radios and every time the VHF or FM radio becomes inoperable it requires that the aircraft be flown to Phu Loi to be repaired. This usually requires half a day to be devoted to this activity.

e. Sling equipment and procedures for sling loading the LOH are different than those used for the Cobra or Huey. It was not until I had to sling out my first LOH that I learned that the Troop did not have the required equipment necessary to accomplish this task. Fortunately one of the other Troops within the Squadron responded and my maintenance crew was able to observe the procedure and equipment required to accomplish this.

5. TRAINING:

    a. Training this Troop in Air Cavalry tactics and techniques while assigned the responsibility for a tactical area of operations was a challenging task. I should point out that if I had not been well versed in these tactics and techniques it would have been an impossible task.

    b. It must be understood that this Troop was pieced together with Brigade Scouts, Gunship Pilots from the Assault Helicopter Battalion, and Scouts and Gunship Pilots from the other Troops of the Squadron. Each of these pilots, while highly motivated and with a great deal of experience, were attempting to perform each Air Cavalry mission as they would have, had they been assigned to their former units. This resulted in a less than desirable performance as a unit. The requirements for leadership and a tactical SOP was paramount. I found it necessary to explain duties, in detail, for every type of operation, for everyone concerned from the Operations Officer to the RTO (Radio Telephone Operator). Those duties I found necessary to explain are contained in enclosure 1.

    c. n an attempt to gain the maximum amount of Air Cavalry experience in the shortest amount of time, the Troop was required to send from one to three teams to the other Troops of the Squadron on a daily basis to receive the benefit of their experience. This did not achieve the results desired. Each Commander has his own way of accomplishing a given tactical task. I found that some procedures that were SOP in some units did not conform to my SOP. This compounded my training problems. In addition to the above, the Troop was struggling to establish its identity as a functioning organization. When my teams worked for the other Troops they were often relegated to the status of a 'new guy', although many of these men had completed a normal tour and were on a six months extension. This had a detrimental effect on morale and again, compounded my training problem.

d. Although I have previously mentioned the lack of an assigned Blue Platoon I must mention it again in this portion of the report. Each Platoon (from D/1-9) received training not only in Air Cavalry tactics but also the Airmobile procedures used within this Troop. I had to be very selective in the locations used to conduct the first insertions with each Platoon. Although they were very quick to grasp my procedures and conducted their ground reconnaissance in a very professional and outstanding manner, it was training and testing of an unknown quantity that was time consuming to the Troop.

6. CONCLUSIONS:

a. In this report I have attempted to highlight the problem areas to be avoided in forming a provisional Air Cavalry Troop. What has not been reflected in this report are the results that have been achieved by this Troop.

b. This Troop was formed to provide an increased reconnaissance capability for the Division. In that respect it has surpassed the expectations of everyone concerned, including myself. This Troop has located the major routes of traffic through our assigned area of responsibility and has located major staging areas for NVA and VC units operating in the DIVARTY AO.

7. RECOMMENDATIONS:

a. That this report be utilized to assist in the formation of future provisional Air Cavalry Troops.

b. Consideration be given to the formation of another Air Cavalry Troop to further increase the Division's capability to find, fix and destroy the enemy within its area of responsibility.

8. LESSONS LEARNED:

a. It is imperative that a General Order designating this unit a provisional Air Cavalry Troop, assigned to the 1st Squadron 9th Cavalry, be issued as soon as possible.

b. That each Air Cavalry Troop receive a minimum of seven UH-1H helicopters and that they be fully equipped, to include the cargo hook.

c. That the manning level of the DS Maintenance Detachment be substantially increased to meet the increased work load.

d. That the proposed provisional unit be given the opportunity to TI the aircraft before Squadron signs for them.

e. That an organic Blue Platoon be assigned to the Troop.

f. That the Provisional Air Cavalry Troop receive LOH and UH-1 H Technical Inspectors and trained line Crew Chiefs prior to receiving the helicopters.

g. A more realistic Basic PLL for the LOH be provided for future troops.

h. That the provisional troop be given one week to organize and conduct training prior to assuming responsibility for a tactical AO.

i. That the Troop work together as a unit and not work with other Air Cavalry Troops.

j. That an experienced Air Cavalry Troop Commander be assigned with the task of organizing and training the Troop.

/s/ Hilbert H. Chole
/t/ HILBERT H. CHOLE
Major Armor
Commanding

ENCLOSURE

1. Tactical SOP

Enclosure 1, Lessons Learned, 20 October 1970

TACTICAL SOP
E TROOP 1st SQUADRON 9th AIR CAVALRY

1. GENERAL: The following procedures are established as this Troop's Standard Operational Procedures.

2. PILOTS:

   a. White Teams will fly during periods of low ceiling.

   (1) Each Scout will carry a map and an SOI (Signal Operating Procedures).

   (2) One Scout will lead the team for half the mission and then the other Scout will assume the lead.

   (3) There will be no high Scout, both will work at the same altitude with the chase Scout flying circles around the lead Scout, 500 - 800 metres away. This insures the lead Scout will have plenty of room to work without worrying about the chase aircraft.

   (4) Before working an area the chase Scout will get their location on the map. Once that is determined they can work the area.

   (5) The chase Scout is responsible for transmitting the spot report and also providing cover for the lead Scout.

   (6) The chase Scout, at the start of the mission, will call OFF to operations and the lead Scout will get clearance from the tower.

   b. Pink Teams are to be the normal method of operation.

   (1) Each Scout is required to carry a map and SOI.

   (2) The weapons aircraft crew assumes responsibility for

determining their location on the map and transmitting all spot reports.

(3) The Scout must know his general location in the AO at all times. Each Scout is required to conduct a detailed map reconnaissance prior to and after each mission. In addition, the pilots are required to memorize specific grid lines i.e. the 40 grid line runs through the testicles, the 50 grid line runs through Phouc Vinh. The 00 grid line is east of Phouc Vinh. In this manner when they are given a location to check, the team can immediately move toward the location while plotting the exact location on the map.

(4) They are to remain a team at all times, i.e. the Scout aircraft can normally remain on station longer than the weapons aircraft. They are to go to the AO and return as a team.

(5) On initial contact with the enemy the Scout will mark with a smoke grenade, engage the area, make an estimate of the situation, and either kill the enemy force or leave the immediate area and call the Red Bird (Cobra) in. After the Weapons aircraft has engaged the area he will clear the Scout back into the area to check it out.

(6) Prior to inserting the Blues, the team selects the LZ and gives a briefing to the lift pilots and the Blue Platoon Leader. This briefing will consist of the following minimum information: Formation the lift will use (single ship, two ships, etc.), Landing direction, situation report, and what direction the Blues are to move (in degrees) after they are inserted.

(7) Spot reports are to be transmitted to Troop Operations every thirty minutes.

(8) When working over Infantry Companies, the Weapons aircraft will also transmit spot reports to the Infantry Battalion Headquarters (every thirty minutes).

(9) General:

(a) All aircraft to be flown the next day will be

preflighted the night before.

(b) The Scout will get tower clearance and the Weapons crew will call OFF to Troop Operations.

(c) If a crew is required to RON (Remain Overnight somewhere else) they are to contact Troop Operations as soon as possible.

(d) All aircraft will be refueled and rearmed prior to parking.

(e) The standard Blue Insertion will proceed as follows:

(1) The team on station will evaluate the enemy situation and terrain, based on their professional judgement they will recommend to the Troop Commander that the Blues be inserted.

(2) When approved, the Lift will proceed to a designated orbit point not more than three minutes flight time from the intended point of insertion.

(3) One Weapons aircraft will escort the lift from the Troop to the orbit point.

(4) The Weapons aircraft crew on station at the intended point of insertion will request a Section of ARA (Aerial Rocket Artillery), brief the lift aircraft on direction of landing, formation, condition of LZ, and enemy situation. The Weapons aircraft crew will control the insertion.

(5) When ARA, the lift, and the one escorting Weapons aircraft are orbiting together, the controlling Weapons aircraft crew will join the lift orbit.

(6) On order of the controlling Weapons aircraft crew, the lift aircraft will leave the orbit point (and start inbound for the LZ).

(7) ARA will fly over the lead lift ship and will

proceed them to the LZ. The two Troop Weapons aircraft will trail the Lift ships, one on either side of the formation.

(8) On base leg into the LZ, the controlling Weapons aircraft crew will direct the Scout to mark the LZ (with a smoke grenade) and have him hold to one side.

(9) On turning final into the LZ, ARA will prep the LZ by expending 50% (of their rocket load). As they are prepping the LZ, the Lift will be on short final. When ARA breaks, the two Troop Weapons aircraft will continue the prep until the lift ships are on the ground.

(10) When the insertion is complete the escorting Weapons aircraft will return to the Troop area.

(11) ARA will remain on station (at a designated orbit point) until it is determined they are no longer required.

(12) The Lift aircraft will laager at a location near the QRF (Quick Reaction Force).

(13) The controlling Weapons aircraft crew will clear the Scout back into the area as soon as practical after the insertion.

3. OPERATIONS SECTION:

    a. Maintain a current situation map.

    b. Maintain a current intelligence map.

    c. Establish reconnaissance boxes within the assigned area of operations. Each reconnaissance box to be 5000 metres by 5000 metres.

    d. Establish an S-2 file to correspond to the reconnaissance boxes. This file will consist of a 1:50000 map with all spot reports from the Troop plotted in ink with a number. A separate sheet of paper will contain the corresponding number with the complete spot report for that point.

  e. Establish flight following.

  f. Ensure we have continuous coverage over the Blues when they are on the ground. This means a team will be sent to the Blue's location every one hour and fifteen minutes.

  g. Ensure spot reports are passed to Squadron in a timely fashion. Acceptable length of time between spot reports is thirty minutes.

  h. Maintain flight records of all personnel on flight status.

  i. Monitor the LNO (Liaison Officer at DIVARTY Hq's) to ensure he has all spot reports and accomplishes assigned duties.

  j. Maintain communication with Squadron and all teams within the AO.

  k. Post all changes to the SOI, and maintain a log on the SOI'S. Each pilot will sign for his SOI and have it secured to his person.

  1. Establish and maintain training records for every man within the Troop.

  m. Conduct briefings at 0700 hours and 1930 hours every day. These briefings will consist of the Troop activities for the day.

  n. Remain abreast of the status of all aircraft throughout the day.

  o. Schedule the teams throughout the day and recommend areas of interest to the Commanding Officer.

  p. Maintain a daily staff journal.

4. LIAISON OFFICER:

a. Perform duties as the Commanding Officer's representative to the supported unit.

b. Advise the supported unit as to the best method of employment for the Troop.

c. When the Blues are to be inserted, accomplish the following:

(1) Obtain clearance to put them in.

(2) Request a Section of ARA and give them the UHF and VHF frequencies the team will be working on.

(3) Obtain the call sign and location of the QRF. Inform Troop Operations if the QRF has its own lift.

(4) Have the Artillery lay a tube in the general location of where the Blues are to be inserted. Obtain the call sign and location of the firing battery.

d. Know the location of all teams within the AO.

e. Keep the supported unit informed as to what the teams are finding.

f. Brief the Troop Operations at the daily supported units briefing.

g. Maintain communications with Troop Operations and the teams in the AO.

TAB F

9TH AIR CAVALRY BRIGADE (PROVISIONAL)

COMBAT AFTER ACTION REPORT
1 SEPTEMBER 1970 - 15 FEBRUARY 1971

RESULTS ACHIEVED BY PROVISIONAL TROOPS

**1ST CAVALRY DIVISION (AIRMOBILE)
PHUOC VINH, SOUTH VIETNAM**

Operational results of E Troop (Provisional) 1-9 Cavalry

Period of time: 1 September 1970 - 30 November 1970 (first 91 days)

Friendly KIA's	2
Friendly WIA's	10
NVA KBH	31
NVA KIA	2
VC KBH	21
VC KIA	2
VC POW/HC	2
DETAINEES	1
IND WEAPONS FOUND	5
IND WEAPONS DESTROYED	3
IND WEAPONS CAPTURED	6
C/S WEAPONS DESTROYED	0
RICE SPOTTED Lbs.	1470
RICE DESTROYED Lbs.	176
DOCUMENTS CAPTURED (inches)	10
CONTACTS MADE	52
CONTACTS WITH RESULTS	24
STRUCTURES DESTROYED	65
BRIDGES DESTROYED	3
SAMPANS DESTROYED	8

Operational Results of F Troop (Provisional) 1-9 Cavalry

Period of time: 9 December 1970 - 25 February 1971 (First 79 days)

Friendly WIA's	1
NVA KBH	3
DETAINEES	3
IND WEAPONS DESTROYED	1
C/S WEAPONS DESTROYED	2
RICE DESTROYED Lbs.	1595
CONTACTS MADE	18
CONTACTS WITH RESULTS	2
STRUCTURES DESTROYED	31
SAMPANS DESTROYED	1
TRUCKS DESTROYED	2

Operational results of E Troop (Provisional) 3-17 Cavalry

Period of time: 27 November 1970 - 16 January 1971 (first 51 days)

DETAINEES	5
RICE DESTROYED Lbs.	18
CONTACTS MADE	12
STRUCTURES DESTROYED	33
SAMPANS DESTROYED	8

TAB G

9TH AIR CAVALRY BRIGADE (PROVISIONAL)

COMBAT AFTER ACTION REPORT
1 SEPTEMBER 1970 - 15 FEBRUARY 1971

**FRAG ORDER #0297 - 2, 3-17 ACS OPCON TO 1 ACD
25 OCTOBER 1970**

**1ST CAVALRY DIVISION (AIRMOBILE)
PHUOC VINH, SOUTH VIETNAM**

                    CG 1ACD PVN RVN
                    CO 1-9 ACS PVN RVN
                    CO 3-17 ACS DAN RVN
            INFO: CG 11 FFV LBN RVN
                    CG 25 INF DIV (US) CCI RVN
                    CO 1 BDE BNH RVN
                    CO 2 BDE SBE RVN
                    CO 3 BDE FSB MACE RVN
                    CO 11 ACR DAN RVN
                    CO DIVARTY PVN RVN (COURIER)
                    CO 1 1 CAG PVN RVN (COURIER)
                    SA 5TH DIV LKE RVN (COURIER)
                    CO 8 ENG PVN RVN (COURIER)
                    CO 13 SIG PVN RVN (COURIER)
                    CO DISCOM BNH RVN
                    CO BHAB BNH RVN
                    CO 14 MIL HIST DET PVN RVN (COURIER)

(CLASSIFICATION) AVDAGT-P

FRAGO #0297 - 2

INFO: CG 1; ADC-A 1; ADC-B 1; CofS 1; G2 1; G2 Opns 1; G3 1; G3 Opns 1; G3 D&T 1; G4 1; G5 1; PMO 1; AIO 1; FSCC 1; ADAO 1; ADE 1; ADSO 1; Cml Off 1; DTO 1; AG (Rear) 1; AG Files 1.

    PHILLIP W. POE, MAJ, AG-3 Plans
              DOWNGRADE AT 3 YEAR INTERVALS
              DECLASSIFIED AFTER 12 YEARS
    MAURICE O. EDWARDS, LTC, GS, AcofS, G3

1. General.

    a. Effective 26 Oct 70, 3-17 ACS (-), consisting of the Squadron Hq's and A and B Troops will become OPCON to 1 ACD.

    b. Central co-ordinating headquarters for Air Cavalry support in the 1 ACD AO will be 1-9 ACS.

c. 1-9 ACS (-), with A, D, and E Troops, will assume OPCON of A/3-17 ACS and provide priority support to the 2nd Bde, DIVARTY and 7th ARVN Regt.

d. 3-17 ACS (-), with B Troop, will assume OPCON of B and C/1-9 ACS and provide priority support to the 1st and 3d Bde's.

e. Both ACS's will remain GS to 1 ACD.

2. Tasks.

   a. 1-9 ACS:

   (1) Continue as the co-ordinating Hqs for air cavalry employment in AO.

   (2) Release OPCON of B and C Troops to 3-17 ACS.

   (3) Assume OPCON of A/3-17 ACS.

   (4) Support 2d Bde, DIVARTY, and 7th ARVN Regt on priority basis.

   b. 3-17 ACS (-)

   (1) Release OPCON of A Troop to 1-9 ACS.

   (2) Assume OPCON B and C/1-9 ACS.

   (3) Support 1st and 3rd Bde's on a priority basis.

   (4) Station A/3-17 Cav at Quan Loi.

3. Co-ordinating Instructions:

   a. DIRLAUTH

   b. OPCON of subordinate air cav troops change on 26 Oct 70

at times and locations mutually agreed upon by CO, 1-9 Cav and CO, 3-17 Cav.

    4. Action addressees acknowledge. PVN 5318/SK 137.

TAB H

9TH AIR CAVALRY BRIGADE (PROVISIONAL)

COMBAT AFTER ACTION REPORT
1 SEPTEMBER 1970 - 15 FEBRUARY 1971

REQUEST TO ESTABLISH A PROVISIONAL AIR CAVALRY BRIGADE
5 NOVEMBER 1970

1ST CAVALRY DIVISION (AIRMOBILE)
PHUOC VINH, SOUTH VIETNAM

AVDAGT-DT (5 November 1970) 1st Ind
SUBJECT: Request to establish a Provisional Air Cavalry Brigade

DA, Headquarters 1st Cavalry Division (Airmobile), APO San Francisco 96490 4 December 1970

TO: Commanding Officer, 1st Squadron 9th Cavalry, 1st Cavalry Division (Airmobile), APO 96490

1. Request contained in basic correspondence is approved.

2. A General Order organizing the 9th Air Cavalry Brigade (Provisional), 1st Cavalry Division (Airmobile) will be published. No personnel augmentation will be provided. The position of Commanding Officer, 9th Air Cavalry Brigade (Provisional) will be filled by the Commanding Officer, 1st Squadron 9th Cavalry.

3. Personnel to establish the proposed Provisional Brigade Headquarters and staff must be provided from authorized assets of the 1st Squadron 9th Cavalry. Selected personnel will function in dual positions to perform duties in both organizations.

FOR THE COMMANDER:

/s/ F.K. Budzyna
/t/ F.K. BUDZYNA
CPT AGC
Asst AG

DEPARTMENT OF THE ARMY
HEADQUARTERS, 1ST SQUADRON, 9TH CAVALRY
(AIRMOBILE)
1ST CAVALRY DIVISION (AIRMOBILE)
APO San Francisco 96490

AVDARS-3   5 November 1970

SUBJECT: Request to establish a Provisional Air Cavalry Brigade

Commanding General
(ATTN: ACofS G3)
1st Air Cav Div (AM)
APO San Francisco 96490

1. Request that a General Order be published establishing a provisional Air Cavalry Brigade within the 1st ACD retroactive to 1 November 1970.

2. It is visualized that the current 1st Squadron, 9th Cavalry Headquarters and staff with slight augmentation would function in the dual capacity as the senior Command and Control headquarters and staff for the Brigade and for the Squadron. This arrangement is currently in effect as a result of 3-17 ACS (-) being attached for tactical operations. Augmentation to the current staff would come from personnel assets currently available or authorized in the 1st Squadron, 9th Cavalry. The one exception would be the assignment of LTC Carl Putnam as DCO for operations upon his arrival in the Division.

3. The mission of the 9th Air Cav Bde (Prov) will be to perform reconnaissance and security for the Division and/or its major subordinate combat elements; to engage in combat as an economy of force unit; and to provide a limited senior Command and Control Headquarters for other combat units (Air Cavalry, Infantry, Artillery) for a specified area of operations or for specified tasks.

4. Task organization is shown at enclosure 1.[8]

5. A proposed organization and grade authorization for the Brigade Headquarters and staff is shown at enclosure 2.[9] Those positions (i.e. Asst S - 1, 2, 3 and 4 and Assistant Staff NCO'S) which could not be manned from existing personnel resources would remain unfilled.

6. Establishment of a provisional Air Cavalry Brigade would provide for a logical tactical grouping and improve the span of control of an organization that currently employs two-fifths of the Divisions total aircraft and approximately 2300 Officers, Warrant Officers, and men in Air Cavalry operations. The prospect of additional provisional Air Cavalry troops (F/1-9 and E/3-17) being organized in the near future would further justify this request. In addition, the formation of such an organization and employment in a combat environment would provide valuable experience and input to the Air Cavalry Combat Brigade scheduled for activation in late FY71 or early FY72 at Fort Hood Texas.

/s/ Robert H. Nevins
/t/ ROBERT H. NEVINS
LTC ARMOR
Commanding

---

[8] Author's Note: Enclosure 1 was missing from my source documents.

[9] Author's Note: Enclosure 2 was missing from my source documents.

TAB I

9TH AIR CAVALRY BRIGADE (PROVISIONAL)

COMBAT AFTER ACTION REPORT
1 SEPTEMBER 1970 - 15 FEBRUARY 1971

MISSION OF THE BRIGADE AND MANNING OF BRIGADE HEADQUARTERS

1ST CAVALRY DIVISION (AIRMOBILE)
PHUOC VINH, SOUTH VIETNAM

Author's Note:: The letter of transmittal for this correspondence was missing from my source documents. This was a follow up document to the request for formation of an Air Cavalry Brigade written by LTC Nevins on 5 November (Tab H).

9th AIR CAV BDE (PROV)

INDEX

TITLE	PAGE
9Th AIR CAV BDE (PROV) MISSION	1
TASK ORGANIZATION	2
STAFF HEADQUARTERS ORGANIZATION	3
S-1 SECTION	4
S-2 SECTION	5
S-3 SECTION	6
S-4 SECTION	7
SAFETY	8
BDE AVIATION MAINTENANCE SECTION	9
COMMO	10
MEDICAL	11

*NOTE: THE CURRENT MTOE FOR A GROUND CAV TROOP, THE AIR CAV TROOP. ENGR CO, AND THE CMBT TRKR PLT ARE ALL APPLICABLE AND ARE AVAILABLE FOR REFERENCE UPON REQUEST. THE MTOE FOR HQ TRP, 9TH CAN BDE (PROV) WILL BE AVAILABLE ON OR ABOUT 10 NOVEMBER 1970.

DEPARTMENT OF THE ARMY
9TH AIR CAV BDE (PROV)
1ST CAVALRY DIVISION (AIRMOBILE)
APO SAN FRANCISCO 96490

AVDARS-3   24 November 1970
SUBJECT: 9TH AIR CAV BDE (PROV)

THE MISSION OF THE 9TH AIR CAV BDE (PROV) WILL BE TO PERFORM RECONNAISSANCE AND SECURITY FOR THE DIVISION OR ITS MAJOR SUBORDINATE COMBAT ELEMENTS; TO ENGAGE IN COMBAT AS AN ECONOMY OF FORCE UNIT; AND TO PROVIDE A LIMITED AIR AND GROUND ANTI-TANK CAPABILITY. IN ADDITION THE BRIGADE WOULD BE CAPABLE OF RECEIVING AND EMPLOYING OTHER COMBAT UNITS (INFANTRY BN, ARTY BTRY) AND ACTING AS A SENIOR COMMAND AND CONTROL HEADQUARTERS FOR A SPECIFIC AREA OF OPERATION.

THE INITIAL EMPLOYMENT WILL BE ONE (1) TROOP GS TO 2ND BDE, ONE (1) TROOP SUPPORTING THE 7TH ARVN REGIMENT WITH INITIAL EMPHASIS ON THE BN BORDER AREA, AND ONE (1) TROOP GS TO DIVARTY WITH A REINFORCEMENT MISSION TO 2ND BDE AND THE 7TH ARVN REGT. IN ADDITION, ONE (1) TROOP WILL BE GS TO 1ST BDE AND INITIALLY TWO (2) TROOPS IN GS OF 3RD BDE.

THE 9TH AIR CAVALRY BRIGADE (PROV) WOULD RETAIN THE CAPABILITY OF REINFORCING ANY AREA IN THE 1ACD AO OR THE 5TH ARVN AO WITH ADDITIONAL AIR CAV ASSETS AS REQUIRED. THE INITIAL EMPLOYMENT AS PREVIOUSLY OUTLINED WOULD INCREASE THE VR IN THE 1 ACD AO BY 25%.

(1)

TASK ORGANIZATION

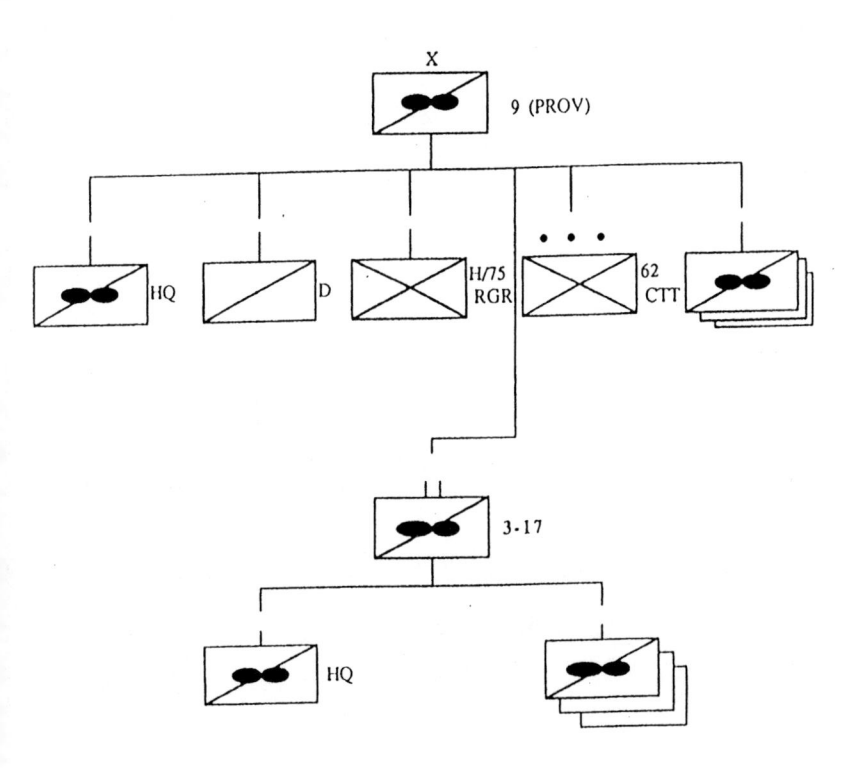

STAFF
HEADQUARTERS ORGANIZATION

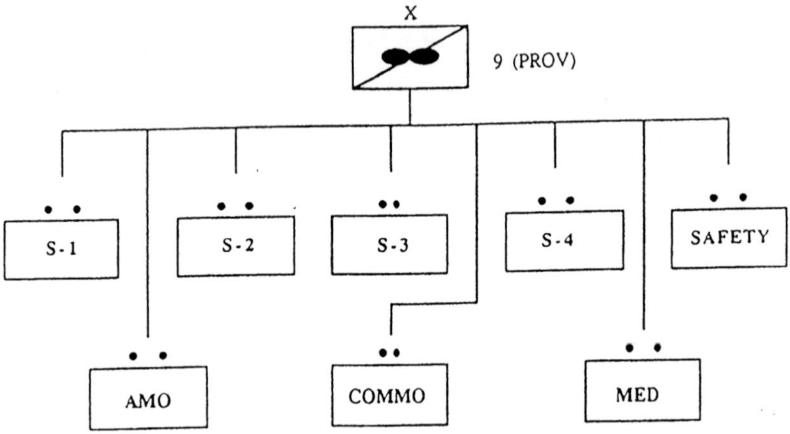
X
9 (PROV)
S-1
S-2
S-3
S-4
SAFETY
AMO
COMMO
MED

COMMAND SECTION

CO	COL	61204	AR
XO	LTC	61204	AR
CSM	E-9	00250	NC

S-1 SECTION

POSITION	MOS	GRADE	REQ
ADJ	2110	MAJ	1
ASSIST ADJ	2110	LT	1
CHAPLAIN	5310	CPT	1
ADMIN SGT	71L50	E-8	1
PERS STAFF NCO	71H40	E-7	1
ADMIN SPEC	71L20	E-5	1
CLERK TYP	71B30	E-5	2
CHAP ASST	71M120	E-5	1
CLERK TYP	71B20	E-4	2
LEGAL CLERK	71D20	E-5	1
MAIL CLERK	71F20	E-4	1
LT TRK DR	11D10	E-3	1

(4)

S-2 SECTION

POSITION	MOS	GRADE	REQ
S-2	9301	MAJ	1
ASST S-2	9301	CPT	1
INTEL SGT	11D50	MSG	1
ASST INTEL SGT	11D40	SFC	1
INTEL ASST	11D20	SP5	1
CLERK TYP	71B30	SP4	1
RTO	11D20	SP4	3
DRAFTSMAN	81A10	SP4	1
LT TRK DRVR	11D10	PFC	1

(5)

S-3 SECTION

POSITION	MOS	GRADE	REQ
S-3	62162	MAJ	1
ASSI S3	62162	CPT	1
S-3 AIR	61204	CPT	1
LNO	61204	LT	3
OPS SGT	11D50	SGM	1
FLT OPS SGT	71P50	MSG	1
CML NCO	54E40	SFC	1
ASST OPS SGT	11D40	SFC	1
ASST FLT OPS SGT	71P40	SSG	1
OPS ASST	11D20	SP5	2
CML OPS ASST	54E20	SP5	1
FLT OPS COOR	71Y20	SP4	2
CLERK TYP	71B30	SP4	2
RTO	11D20	SP4	3
DRAFTSMAN	81A10	SP4	1
LT TRK DRVR	11D10	PFC	3

(6)

S-4 SECTION

POSITION	MOS	GRADE	REQ
S-4	64020	MAJ	1
ASST S-4	64020	CPT	1
PBO	761A0	WO	1
S-4 SGT	76Y50	MSG	1
PROP BOOK NCO	76T40	SSG	2
CLERK	76Y20	SP4	2
SUPPLY SGT	76Y20	SP4	1
DRIVER (HVY)	64B20	PFC	1
DRIVER (LT)	64A20	PFC	1
SUPPLY MAN	64B20	PFC	2
SUPPORT PLT PLT CMDR	0400	CPT	1
PLT SGT	76Y40	PSG	1
AMMO SGT	55B40	SSG	1
FACILITIES NCO	57G40	SSG	1
AMMO HANDLER	55A20	SP4	2
CLERK	71B20	SP4	1
DRIVER	64A10	PFC (7)	1

SAFETY SECTION

POSITION	MOS	GRADE	REQ
AVN SAFETY OFF	07423	CPT	1
SIP AH-1G	100E	WO	1
SIP UH-1H	100B	WO	1
SIP OH-6A	100B	WO	1
CLERK TYP	71B30	SP4	1

(8)

BRIGADE AVIATION MAINTENANCE SECTION

POSITION	MOS	GRADE	REQ
AVN MAINT OFF	64821	MAJ	1
ASST AVN MAINT OFF	64821	CPT	1
AVN MAINT SUPPLY	67Z50	MSG	1
AVN MAINT TECH	671C	WO	1
TECH SUPP SUPV	76T40	SFC	1
AVN TECH INSP	67W20	SP6	1
RECORDS SPEC	71T20	SP5	2
AVN PARTS SPEC	76T20	SP5	1
AVN PARTS APP	76A10	PFC	1
AVN MAINT APP	67A10	PFC	1

(9)

COMMUNICATION SECTION

POSITION	MOS	GRADE	REQ
PLT HQ			
SIGNAL OFF	0205	MAJ	1
COMMO PLT LDR	0205	LT	1
COMMO CHIEF	31G50	MSG	1
RADIO MECH	31B20	SP5	2
RADIO MECH	31B20	SP4	3
COMMUNICATION CENTER AND INSTALLATION SECTION			
SECT LDR	31G40	SFC	1
WIRE CHIEF	36K40	SSG	1
TEAM CHIEF	36K40	SGT	3
SR WIREMAN	36K20	SP4	3
WIREMAN	36K20	PFC	9
SR SWBD OPR	72C20	SP4	2
SWBD OPR	72C20	PFC	4
COMMO CNTR SUPV	72B40	SGT	1
CRYPTO MAINT SPEC	72B20	SGT	1
CRYPTO CLRK	72B20	SP4	1
MESSENGER	72B20	PFC	2
COMMO CNTR SPEC	72B20	SP4	2
RADIO SECTION			
SEC CHIEF	05C40	SFC	1
RATT CHIEF	05C40	SSG	1
RATT TM CHIEF	05C40	SGT	7
RATT OPER	05C20	SP4	14
SR RADIO OPER	05B20	SP4	3
RADIO OPER	05B20	PFC	3

(10)

MEDICAL SECTION

POSITION	MOS	GRADE	REQ
FLT SURG	3160	CPT	1
MED SEC LDR	3506	LT	1
NCOIC	91B40	E-7	1
MED LAB SPEC	92B20	E-4	1
MED ASST	91C20	E-5	1
SR AIDMAN	91B20	E-5	1
AMB DRVR	91B20	E-4	1
AMB ATTENDANT	91A10	E-3	1
LT TRK DRVR	91A10	E-3	1
MED AIDMAN	91B20	E-4	9
PHARMACIST	91020	E-4	1
X-RAY TECH	91920	E-4	1
CLERK TYP	91B20	E-4	1

(11)

TAB J

9TH AIR CAVALRY BRIGADE
(PROVISIONAL)

COMBAT AFTER ACTION REPORT
1 SEPTEMBER 1970 - 15 FEBRUARY 1971

MESSAGE FORMING 9TH AIR CAVALRY BRIGADE
5 DECEMBER 1970

1ST CAVALRY DIVISION (AIRMOBILE)
PHUOC VINH, SOUTH VIETNAM

MESSAGE COVER SHEET

CLASSIFICATION
051410Z DEC 1970

FROM: CG 1 ACD PVN RVN
TO: CO 9TH AIR CAV BDE (PROV) PVN RVN
CO 3RD SQDN, 1 TFH CAV DAN RVN
INFO: CG II FFV LBN RVN
CG 25TH INF DIV (US) CCI RVN
CG 5TH ARVN DIV LKE RVN
CO 1ST BDE BNH RVN
CO 2ND BDE SBE RVN
CO 3RD BDE FSB MACE RVN
CO DIVARTY PVN RVN (COURIER)
CO DISCOM BNH RVN
CO 11TH CAG PVN RVN (COURIER)
CO 1-9 CAV PVN RVN (COURIER)
CO 11TH ACR DAN RVN PSA BINH DUONG (P) PHU GUONG RVN (COURIER)
SA BIEN HOA SECTOR BNH RVN (COURIER)
CO BHAB BNH RVN
CO 13TH SIG PVN RVN (COURIER)
CO MIL HIST PVN RVN (COURIER)
CO 15TH MED PVN RVN (COURIER)

DISTR: CG 1; ADC-A 1; ADC-B 1; CofS 1; G1 1; G2 Cons 1; G3 1; G3 Cons 1; G2 1; G3 D&T 5; G4 1; PMO 1; ALO 1; FSCO 1; ADAO 1; ADE 1; ADSO 1; Cml Off 1; AG (Rear) 1; AG files 1; DTO 1.
MAURICE O. EDMONDS, LTC, GS, ACofS, G3

DOWNGRADED AT 3 YEAR INTERVALS
DECLASSIFIED AFTER 12 YEARS
DOD DIR 5200.1 0

/s/ F.K. Budzyna
/t/ F.K. BUDZYNA, CPT, AGC, ASST AG
CLASSIFICATION

MESSAGE

CLASSIFICATION OF3398

AVDAGT-DT

FRAGO #339 - 2

1. GENERAL:

9TH AIR CAVALRY BDE (PROV) HAS BEEN FORMED TO CONTROL OPERATIONS OF ALL AIR CAVALRY ASSETS AVAILABLE TO 1ACD.

2. TASKS:

A. 9TH AIR CAVALRY BDE (PROV): ASSUMES OPCON 1-9 ACS AND 3-17 (-) ACS EFFECTIVE 080600H DEC 1970.

B. 1 SQDN 9TH CAV: REVERT OPCON 9TH AIR CAV BDE (PROV) EFFECTIVE 080600H DEC 1970.

C. 3D SQDN, 17TH CAV (-): REVERT OPCON 9TH AIR CAV BDE (PROV) EFFECTIVE 080600H DEC 1970.

3. CO-ORDINATING INSTRUCTIONS: DIRLAUTH

4. ACTION ADRESSEES ACKNOWLEDGE PVN 5326SK 138

GP-4

TAB K

9TH AIR CAVALRY BRIGADE (PROVISIONAL)

COMBAT AFTER ACTION REPORT
1 SEPTEMBER 1970 - 15 FEBRUARY 1971

GENERAL ORDER AND MESSAGE FORMING F TROOP
11 DECEMBER 1970

1ST CAVALRY DIVISION (AIRMOBILE)
PHUOC VINH, SOUTH VIETNAM

DEPARTMENT OF THE ARMY
HEADQUARTERS, 1ST CAVALRY DIVISION (AIRMOBILE)
APO San Francisco 96490

GENERAL ORDERS
NUMBER 21505						11 December 1970
TC 001. Following Action Directed

F TROOP (PROVISIONAL), 1ST SQUADRON 9TH CAVALRY
APO San Francisco 96490

Action: Organize
Assigned to : 1st Squadron, 9th Cavalry
Mission: To perform reconnaissance and to provide security for combat elements and to engage in combat as an economy of force unit.
Effective date: 8 December 1970
Authorized strength: N/A
Structure strength: N/A
Morning reports: In accordance with paragraph 1 - 8, AR 680 - 1
Authority: Verbal orders of the Commanding General
Special Instructions: Personnel will remain assigned to parent organization and will be attached to F Troop (Provisional) 1-9 Cavalry for administration, rations, quarters, and military justice. Promotion authority remains with Commanding Officer of parent organization. Promotions will be effected against authorized position vacancies of the parent unit.

FOR THE COMMANDER
OFFICIAL:				G.E. NEWMAN
					Colonel, GS
					Chief of Staff

/s/ Gorden E. Grant
/t/ GORDEN E. GRANT
    LTC, AGC
    ADJUTANT GENERAL

Annex A: Space authorizations for F Troop (Provisional)
DISTRIBUTION:
A Plus
5-ACofS, G3
10-1st Sqdn, 9th Cav

ANNEX A (Space authorizations for F Troop Provisional) to GENERAL ORDERS NUMBER 21505

1. The following spaces are provided for F Troop (Provisional except as indicated in paragraph a.

UNIT MTOE	PAR	LINE	DESCRIPTION	GRADE	MOS	NO
a. D Co, 229 AHB 1-157T			All except the following which are provided 2-20 Arty Bn.			
	04	01	SEC CMDR	LT	01981	3
		02	HELI PILOT	WO	100E	3
		03	AH-1G Crew Chf	E5	67N2F	3
	06	05	ACFT ARMORER	E4	45J20	2
b. 571st TRANS 55-570GP		01	ALL SPACES			
c. E/82d Arty 6-702TPOL	04	01	SECTLDR	LT	01193	1
		02	ROTARY WING AV	WO	100BO	3
		03	OH-6A Crew Chf	E5	67V20	6
d. 3d BDE 67-42TP03	08	04	ROTARY WING AV	WO	100BO	2
		08	OH-6A Crew Chf	E5	67V20	2
e. 11THGS CO 1-102TPO1	03	01	SECT LDR	LT	01981	1
		02	ROTARY WING AV	WO	100BO	3
		03	OH-6A Crew Chf	E5	67V20	4

2. SUMMATION:

LOSING UNIT	OFF	WO	EM
3RD BDE		2	2
D CO, 229TH AHB	13	10	87
E/82D ARTY	1	3	6
11TH GS CO	1	3	4
571ST TRANS DET	1	1	36
TOTAL	16	19	135

MESSAGE COVER SHEET
FROM: CG 1 ACD PVN RVN
To: CO 1 1 CAG PVN RVN (COURIER)
CO DIVARTY PVN RVN (COURIER)
CO 1-9TH CAV PVN RVN (COURIER)
CO DISCOM BNH RVN (COURIER)
INFO: CO 1 BDE BNH RVN (COURIER)
CO 2 BDE SBE RVN (COURIER)
CO 3 BDE FSB MACE RVN (COURIER)

CLASSIFICATION
AVDAGT-DT
FRAGO #0339-1

1. GENERAL:

1 ACD EFFECTS INTERNAL REALIGNMENT OF ASSETS TO PROVIDE ADDITIONAL VR CAPABILITY WITHIN AO. AVIATION ASSETS FROM 11TH CAG AND DIVARTY WILL BE PROVIDED TO 1-9TH CAV.

2. TASKS:

A. 1-9TH CAVALRY

(1) EFFECT ATTACHMENT OF D CO (-), 229TH AVN BN TO REINFORCE PRESENT VISUAL RECONNAISSANCE CAPABILITY.

(2) ORGANIZE AND TRAIN F TROOP (PROVISIONAL) TO BE OPERATIONAL NLT 15 DEC 70.

B. 11TH CAG

(1) PROVIDE FOUR (4) OH-6A AIRCRAFT TO F TROOP (PROVISIONAL) 1-9TH CAVALRY.

MAURICE O. EDMONDS, LTC, GS, ACofS, G3
DOWNGRADE AT THREE YEAR INTERVALS
DECLASSIFIED AFTER 12 YEARS
DOD DI R 5200.1 0
/s/ F.K. HUDZYTA, CAPT, AGC, Asst AG

(2) DETACH CO D (-), 229TH AVN BN TO 1-9TH CAVALRY EFFECTIVE 080600H DEC 1970.

(3) PROVIDE SIX (6) AH-1G AIRCRAFT TO DIVARTY.

C. DIVARTY

(1) RECEIVE SIX (6) AH-1G AIRCRAFT FROM 11TH CAG

(2) PROVIDE FOUR (4) OH-6A TO F TROOP (PROVISIONAL) 1-9 CAVALRY.

(3) PROVIDE ESCORT AIRCRAFT SUPPORT T0 11TH CAG ON A MISSION BASIS AS REQUIRED, EFFECTIVE 070600H DEC 70.

D. DISCOM: PROVIDE LOGISTICAL SUPPORT TO INCLUDE PRIMARY DS MAINTENANCE FOR OH-6A AIRCRAFT IN F TROOP (PROVISIONAL) 1-9TH CAVALRY.

3. CO-ORDINATING INSTRUCTIONS.

A. THIS FRAGO SUPERSEDES FRAGO #0338-1

B. DIRLAUTH

C. ANNEX A, PERSONNEL ADMINISTRATION

D. ANNEX B, LOGISTICS[10]

E. AIRCRAFT WILL BE PROVIDED WITH CREWS AND EQUIPMENT AS OUTLINED IN ANNEXES A AND B.

F. TRANSFER OF PERSONNEL AND EQUIPMENT IS EFFECTIVE 080600H DEC 1971

---

[10] Author's Note: This annex was missing from my source documents.

4. ACKNOWLEDGE PVN 5326/SK 138

GP4

ANNEX A (PERSONNEL ADMINISTRATION) TO 1 ACD FRAGO #0339 - 1

1. GENERAL: PERSONNEL WILL REMAIN ASSIGNED TO THEIR PARENT ORGANIZATION. THEY WILL BE ATTACHED TO F TROOP (PROVISIONAL) FOR ADMINISTRATION, RATIONS, QUARTERS AND MILITARY JUSTICE.

2. PROMOTIONS: ENLISTED PROMOTION ALLOCATIONS WILL BE PROVIDED TO THE COMMANDING OFFICER 1-9 CAVALRY. PROMOTIONS WILL BE MADE AGAINST AUTHORIZED POSITION VACANCIES OF THE PARENT UNITS.

3. REPLACEMENTS

a. OFFICER ASSIGNMENTS WILL BE DETERMINED BY G1.

b. ENLISTED REPLACEMENTS WILL BE ASSIGNED BY THE AG, TO PARENT UNITS AND ATTACHED DIRECTLY TO TROOP LEVEL.

4. STRENGTHS RECORDS AND REPORTS

a. IN THE EVENT OF ANY ACTION (KIA, WIA, DEROS, AWOL ETC.) WHICH AFFECTS THE ATTACHED STRENGTH OF F TROOP (PROVISIONAL), THE INDIVIDUAL(S) CONCERNED WILL BE RELEASED FROM ATTACHED STATUS AND RETURNED TO HIS PARENT ORGANIZATION FOR FURTHER ADMINISTRATIVE PROCESSING IN ACCORDANCE WITH APPLICABLE DIRECTIVES.

b. THE COMMANDING OFFICER, F TROOP (PROVISIONAL), WILL BE RESPONSIBLE FOR INITIATING REQUESTS FOR ORDERS FOR RELEASE OF PERSONNEL FROM ATTACHED STATUS AND RETURN TO THEIR PARENT ORGANIZATION.

c. THE COMMANDING OFFICER F TROOP (PROVISIONAL) WILL INITIATE MORNING REPORTS, FOR CONTROL PURPOSES. THEY WILL BE MAINTAINED IN ACCORDANCE WITH THE PROVISIONS OF PARAGRAPH 1 - 8, AR 680 - 1.

d. PERSONNEL DAILY SUMMARIES WILL BE PREPARED AND FORWARDED IN ACCORDANCE WITH STANDARD PROCEDURES THROUGH THE COMMANDING OFFICER, 1-9 CAVALRY.

e. THE DIVISION ADJUTANT GENERAL WILL MAINTAIN A PERSONNEL INFORMATION ROSTER INDICATING SPECIFIC PARAGRAPH AND LINE NUMBER OF THE PARENT UNIT MTOE TO WHICH PERSONNEL ATTACHED TO F TROOP (PROV) ARE ASSIGNED. REPLACEMENT PERSONNEL WILL NOT BE ASSIGNED TO THESE LINE DELETED POSITIONS WHICH ARE RESERVED FOR F TROOP ATTACHED PERSONNEL

5. INDIVIDUAL PERSONNEL ACTIONS: THE FOLLOWING PERSONNEL BY HCS 17PE WILL BE ATTACHED AS INDICATED.

Author's Note: This was the last page of my source documents.

GLOSSARY OF ACRONYMS

1 ACD	1st Air Cavalry Division
ACR	Armored Cavalry Regiment
ADP	Automatic Data Processing
AFA	Aerial Field Artillery
AO	Area of Operations
ARVN	Army of the Republic of South Vietnam
ASP	Ammunition Supply Point
BDA	Bomb Damage Assessment
BLUES	An Aero Rifle Platoon
CAG	Combat Aviation Group
CHICOM	Chinese Communist
Chieu Hois	Surrendered enemy personnel
CO	Commanding Officer
COSVN	Corps Support for Vietnam (NVA)
CP	Command Post
CTT	Combat Tracker Teams
DIVARTY	Division Artillery
DOC	Date Of Capture

DZ	Drop Zone
FRAGO	Fragmentary Order
FSB	Fire Support Base
G2	Intelligence (Division Level)
GVN	Government of South Vietnam
HHT	Headquarters, Headquarters Troop
INTSUM	Intelligence Summary
KBAFA	Killed by Aerial Field Artillery
KBARTY	Killed by Artillery
KBAS	Killed by Air Strike
KBH	Killed by Helicopter
KCS	"Kit Carson Scout" (Vietnamese, probably former VC, working for US forces)
KIA	Killed in Action
LNO	Liaison Officer
LOH	Light Observation Helicopter
LTLIA	Local Tactical Lines of Infiltration Area (NVA)
LZ	Landing Zone
MACV	Military Assistance Command, Vietnam
MIA	Missing In Action

MR	Military Region
MTI	Moving Target Indicator
MTOE	Modified Table of Organization and Equipment
NVA	North Vietnamese Army
NVAC	North Vietnamese Captured
NVAS	North Vietnamese Surrendered
OJT	On the Job Training, i.e. no formal training
OPCON	Operational Control
OPLAN	Operational Plan
OPORD	Operational Order
ORGANICS	Weapons mounted on the aircraft rather than fire power from some other source.
PINK TEAM	One Cobra Helicopter & one Light Observation Helicopter working together.
POL	Fuel and Lubricants
POW	Prisoner Of War
PZ	Pick-up Aone
QRF	Quick Reaction Force
RPG	Rocket Propelled Grenade
RR	Recoilless Rifle

RRF	Ready Reaction Force
RSG	Rear Services Group (NVA)
RTAVF	Royal Thai Army, Vietnam Forces
S2	Staff Intelligence (Battalion Level)
SOP	Standard Operating Procedure
TAC Air	Tactical Air Support
TAOR	Tactical Area Of Responsibility
TF	Task Force
TOC	Tactical Operations Center, or, Time Of Capture
VC	Vietcong
VCC	Vietcong Captured
VCS	Vietcong Surrendered
VHF	Very High Frequency
VR	Visual Reconnaissance
WHITE BIRD	OH-6 Scout Helicopter
WIA	Wounded In Action